PROSPECTS FOR EMPLOYMENT

A TORY VIEW

PROSPECTS FOR EMPLOYMENT

A TORY VIEW

Adam Butler MP *(Bosworth)*
Richard Hornby MP *(Tonbridge)*
Tom King MP *(Bridgwater)*
Cecil Parkinson MP *(Enfield West)*
Timothy Raison MP *(Aylesbury)*
Nicholas Scott MP *(Paddington South)*
Christopher Tugendhat MP *(Cities of London and Westminster)*

Edited by Timothy Raison

CONSERVATIVE POLITICAL CENTRE

In common with other CPC publications, this pamphlet is a personal contribution by the authors to discussion and not an official Party pronouncement. Nor does each of the authors necessarily agree with everything in the pamphlet.

The authors would like to acknowledge their debt to those of their Parliamentary colleagues who contributed substantially to this pamphlet, but were precluded from signing it by their appointment to the Government, while the pamphlet was in its final stages of preparation.

CPC No. 504

Published by the Conservative Political Centre, 32 Smith Square, London SW1 and printed by C. Nicholls and Company Ltd The Philips Park Press, Manchester, M11 4AU

First published June 1972
ISBN 85070 500 2

Contents

Introduction

IN THE COMMONS' DEBATE on unemployment on 24th January 1972, the Prime Minister said, 'We have a kind of unemployment that we have not had before, either before 1939 or since 1945 – the combination of a high rate of inflation, which is now lowering, with a high level of unemployment. This is unique in British experience. . . The plain fact with which we are faced is that we are securing today the same production – in fact, slightly more – as two years ago, using 400,000 fewer to do it.'

In an earlier debate, on 23rd November 1971, Mr Enoch Powell had made the same point in a way which, as he was prepared to admit, challenged the economic purism for which he is famous. 'The coincidence of an unparalleled rise in unemployment with an inflation unchallenged in its severity forces us to revise the philosophies upon which nearly all of us have operated for the past thirty years.'

Unemployment as it exists today is a phenomenon, both political and economical. It is perhaps possible to explain what is happening, as this pamphlet tries to do. But the fact remains that its coming has taken us unawares. Certainly, it caught officialdom unawares: Whitehall took a long time before it was prepared to acknowledge that something out of the ordinary was happening and that the problem was not simply lack of demand. Equally, for all the talk of shake-out and technological improvements, the economists do not seem to have been much quicker to assess the trend. In fact, some of us in politics were even able to hold for a while the suspicion that we were intellectual pace-setters – an unusual experience.

But perhaps that conveys a sense of certainty on our part which would be out of place. We may *know* that something different is under way. We can only *speculate* as to exactly what it is and what to do about it. Good pamphlets, like good trumpets, should sound a note of rollicking certainty. This one, we fear, will sometimes seem tentative.

No matter. We know that at least we are looking at crucial questions about the nature of our economy and our society – as well as, more specifically, about those people who are either experiencing the demoralisation and hardship of unemployment, or who would experience them if the wrong policies were adopted. Our aim is to stimulate our fellow Tories to probe these questions deeply; and, having probed, to act.

PART ONE

THE PROBLEM

CHAPTER ONE

What is happening?

UP TO 1966, the pattern of post-war unemployment was remarkably constant. The percentage of those out of work ranged between 1 per cent and 2 per cent and only rarely and temporarily exceeded 2 per cent. The figure for men exceeded these levels slightly but it only rose above 3 per cent in the year 1963, falling in the following three years to below 2 per cent. By 1965 it looked as if this pattern was assuming a degree of permanency and in that year the National Plan forecast a continuing low level of unemployment coupled with industrial expansion which would result in a manpower deficiency of 400,000 workers in 1970. **But in 1966 the post war pattern started to change and the exact opposite to the National Plan predictions has now come about.**

Since 1966 the annual average level of unemployment in Great Britain (excluding Northern Ireland) has risen constantly.

TABLE ONE

	Total		Men		Women	
	Nos. (000s)	%	*Nos. (000s)*	%	*Nos. (000s)*	%
1966	360	1·5	285	1·9	75	0·9
1967	560	2·4	452	3·0	108	1·3
1968	564	2·4	474	3·2	90	1·1
1969	559	2·4	476	3·3	83	1·0
1970	603	2·6	514	3·6	89	1·0
1971	807	3·5	682	4·0	125	1·5

The level for the last months of 1971 was higher than the

estimated average for the whole year and in January 1972 reached a total of 978,000 or 4.3 per cent.

This pattern is confirmed by the number of workers in jobs over the last ten years in the whole of the UK including Northern Ireland. For the purposes of comparison the month of June is taken in each year, as in this month there is a physical count of national insurance cards.

TABLE TWO

	Total employees in employment	Value of GDP £m (*at constant factor*)	GDP for employee in employment £
1960	22,500,000	24,369	1,096
1965	23,600,000	29,030	1,229
1970	22,900,000	32,232	1,408
1971	22,500,000	N.K.	N.K.

During the first five years of the decade, new jobs were being created at about the rate of nearly 200,000 a year. In the second five years, jobs were disappearing at about 100,000 a year; and in the last year there was a sharp drop of over 400,000 jobs. At the same time, the Gross Domestic Product of the country was rising. Whereas in 1965, 23·6 million workers produced £29,000m, in 1970 400,000 fewer produced £32,000m.

The pattern over the last five years has therefore been one of rising unemployment, accompanied by growth of output which has been achieved by some striking improvements in productivity. The position can be summarised in the table opposite which shows the annual percentage increases.

Over the last five years the growth in output has not been keeping pace with the improvements in productivity. Management throughout the country has been seeking out new ways of producing more goods with fewer workers. This efficiency drive has been given added impetus by the squeeze on profits, liquidity problems and the high level of wage settlements.

This process, which was described by Harold Wilson as the 'shake-out', began in 1966 and was undoubtedly accelerated by the introduction of Selective Employment Tax. The effect of this was particularly noticeable in the construction industry. Industry in the private sector has made some striking productivity gains and some case studies are included later in this pamphlet. One of the pace setters, GEC, after its merger with English Electric in 1968, has reduced its work force from 228,000 to 195,000 in 1971 while increasing both its sales and profits.

The jobs that have been lost are mainly in the manufacturing industries, but service industries have also shed

TABLE THREE

	% improvement in:			
	productivity		output	employment
	1960–65	*1965–70*	*1965–70*	
Whole economy	2·2	2·8	2·3	–0·6
Manufacturing	2·9	3·0	2·5	–0·5
Mining	4·0	6·3	–4·0	–8·2
Agriculture	6·7	5·8	1·8	–4·0
Service industries				
Transport	3·1	4·2	3·3	–0·9
Public utilities	4·0	6·3	4·9	–1·3
Construction	0·8	3·2	0·2	–2·9
Distribution	1·2	3·3	1·5	–1·8
Other services	0·8	1·3	0·8	0·5
Insurance/Banking	0·2	2·3	5·3	3·0
Public administration	—	—	2·2	2·2

labour. The table opposite lists all the people working in services both in the public and private sector. **The major area which has provided a constant and significant increase in jobs over ten years is the public sector and the greatest rise has been in the education and medical services** – from 1,676,000 to 2,455,000. These together with public administration (with which is classified defence) are the fastest growing areas and will provide in the future the greatest opportunities for more employment.

The private service sector increased its work-force in 1960–1965, but in 1965–1970 there was a loss of 349,000 jobs. The only areas of significant employment that have grown consistently over the last decade are insurance, banking and finance, and professional and scientific services. The distributive trades have decreased their work-force, reflecting the growth of self-service and improved productivity in retailing and wholesaling. One feature that is quite striking is that in spite of a great increase in tourism in the 60s and the building of many new hotels, the number of people working in the catering and hotels industry was exactly the same in 1970 as it was in 1960.

These figures cast doubt upon optimistic assessments about job opportunities in the service industries. These industries are just as conscious of labour-saving techniques as manufacturing industries, and moreover many of the opportunities which they will provide in the future will be for women and for part-time workers.

All parts of the country have experienced rising unemployment. The regions which had high levels of unemployment in 1965 have higher levels today but the proportional increase has been in line with the increase in other parts of the country, and sometimes less. This can be measured by a device known as the Unemployment

TABLE FOUR
SERVICE INDUSTRIES EMPLOYMENT

Public sector	*1960 (000s)*	*1965 (000s)*	*1970 (000s)*	*1960–70 % change*
Gas, electricity, water	377	418	390	+3·5
Transport, air, port	1,289	1,250	1,156	−10·3
Educational and medical	1,676	2,056	2,455	+31·7
Public administration and defence	1,285	1,338	1,431	+11·3
	4,627	5,062	5,432	+17·4

10-year total increase: 805,000
5-year total increase: 370,000

Private sector	*1960*	*1965*	*1970*	*1960–70 % change*
Private road transport, haulage	645	676	679	+ 5·3
Distributive trades	2,833	3,021	2,706	− 4·5
Insurance, banking, finance	546	645	964	+76·6
Professional and scientific services	340	406	432	+27·0
Miscellaneous services				
Cinema, theatre, radio	132	131	120	− 9·1
Sport	52	68	66	+26·9
Betting	38	54	59	+55·3
Catering and hotels	577	621	577	—
Laundries	128	124	83	−35·2
Dry cleaning	45	48	29	−35·6
Motor repairs, filling stations	358	442	407	+13·7
Repair of shoes	18	15	7	−61·2
Hairdressing	86	110	87	+ 1·2
Private domestic service	282	212	101	−64·2
Other services	283	402	309	+ 9·2
	6,363	6,975	6,626	+ 4·1

10-year total increase: 263,000
5-year total decrease: 349,000

Multiplier, which compares the percentage unemployed in a particular region with the national percentage. If for example the unemployment rate in the North was twice the national average then the unemployment multiplier for the North would be two.

TABLE FIVE

	North	*Wales*	*Scotland*
1965	1·85	1·9	2·15
1966	1·7	1·95	1·95
1967	1·75	1·75	1·7
1968	1·95	1·7	1·6
1969	2·0	1·7	1·55
1970	1·85	1·5	1·65
1971 (*9 months only*)	1·7	1·4	1·75

These figures indicate that in relation to what is happening in the rest of the country the regions with the exception of Scotland from 1969 to 1971 were not suffering proportionately more and indeed the relative position of Wales has steadily improved. Areas where hitherto unemployment has been negligible, like the Midlands, now have high levels.

One of the features of the rise in unemployment in 1971 was the increase in the number of school leavers who did not get a job. In January 1972 there were 10,000 school leavers remaining unemployed compared to 5,500 a year

TABLE SIX

	July 1969		*July 1971*	
Age	*No. (000s)*	*% of total*	*No. (000s)*	*% of total*
65 and over	1·8	—	1·8	—
60 and over	87·8	21	107·0	17
55 and over	127·6	30	157·0	25
50 and over	157·3	37	200·0	32

earlier – an increase of nearly 100 per cent in a period when the overall level of unemployment had risen by under 50 per cent. **Older people have been rather better at keeping their jobs.** This can be seen in the number of men over 50 who are unemployed.

Although the number of men over fifty out of work has gone up 43,000 this represented a proportional drop in the total number of unemployed from 37 per cent to 32 per cent. **The age group which has experienced the largest proportional increase in unemployment is 18–24 years.** The middle group from 24–50 have remained at the same relative level.

In the early sixties it was commonplace to read articles by economists urging the introduction of a pay roll tax. This was seen as the only way to jerk British management into using its labour more efficiently. Now not a voice is raised extolling a pay roll tax: indeed one is hearing the case for a 'job payment subsidy' paid by the Government to companies which take on more workers than they need. Managers have learnt to live with smaller pay rolls and there seems little evidence that they will return to their old habits.

There is a real likelihood that one factor making employers reluctant to employ more labour will be the growing burden of labour costs over and above wages and salaries which will be accentuated if we follow EEC trends. The following table gives wages and salaries of all employees as a proportion of total labour costs in manufacturing industry in Great Britain and the EEC countries at various dates between 1962 and 1969. 'Wages and salaries' include payment for days not worked, bonuses and tips, plus payments in kind in 1966, 1968 and 1969 but not in earlier years. The remaining labour costs are given as a percentage in parentheses. These costs comprise:

national insurance contributions or statutory social security contributions, net selective employment tax when and where applicable, net provision for redundancy, private social welfare payments, subsidised services such as catering, training and other labour costs (excluding wage and salary costs which are included in 'wages and salaries').

TABLE SEVEN

percentages

	1962–64	*1964*	*1966*	*1968*	*1969*
Great Britain		91·8(8·2)		91(9)	
West Germany	83·4(16·6)		83(17)		83(17)
France	71·1(28·9)		72(28)		75(25)
Italy	67·9(32·1)		71(29)		70(30)
Netherlands	81·1(18·9)		80(20)		77(23)
Belgium	80·6(19·4)		80(20)		80(20)
Luxembourg	82·0(18·0)		85(15)		84(16)

In December 1971, the director-general of the Engineering Employers Federation said that despite the shake-out the industry had a lot of spare capacity which would allow an increase of 15–20 per cent in output without increasing its labour force. Regular surveys of employment prospects are carried out by Taylor-Nelson for the *Financial Times* and *ad hoc* surveys are carried out by various Sunday newspapers – all of these re-affirm the same conclusion – **'faster growth, slower job creation'.**

Between the first half of 1971 and the first half of 1972, the economy grew by 3·9 per cent. This of itself did not create any jobs as it was accompanied by a substantial gain in productivity above the growth rate. Although some industries expect a continuing and comparable rate of productivity increase over the next year or two – and some have indicated that they expect their labour forces to be contained – it is reasonable to plan for 1972/3 and 1973/4 for a slight fall back in productivity improvement to 3 per cent a year. Allowing for a 4½ per cent annual growth rate, it can be expected that in 1972/3 the need first to take up slack will result only in a small reduction in unemployment.

1973/4, on the other hand, will be effected not only by this net growth (i.e. adjusted for productivity increases) which should create 150,000 to 200,000 jobs but also by the once-for-all reduction in the labour force of about 200,000 due to the raising of the school leaving age. This points to an unemployment figure in the range of 600,000 to 650,000 in the autumn of 1973.

Later chapters will give greater detail; but the overall trend seems clear.

CHAPTER TWO

Demand or shake-out?

THE LAST CHAPTER showed that industrial employment has been declining steadily since 1966. To what extent has this been caused by demand factors and to what extent by 'shake-out'?

The first important demand factor was the decision by the Labour Government, after two years in office, to put all its emphasis on defending the country's external trade position and its currency. As a result, the Government took the first steps towards what subsequently proved to be the most prolonged squeeze on internal demand and the most severe credit squeeze since the war. The following table from the OECD Survey for 1971 shows how successful the Government was in restraining consumer expenditure – a major factor in demand.

TABLE EIGHT
REAL CONSUMERS' EXPENDITURE
3-year average growth rates

Three years to	1959	3·0	Three years to	1965	3·3
	1960	3·6		1966	2·5
	1961	3·5		1967	2·1
	1962	2·8		1968	2·1
	1963	2·9		1969	1·5
	1964	3·3		1970	1·8

The rate of increase in 1969 was less than half that of 1965 and 1970 showed little improvement.

This slowing down in demand was a major factor in producing the substantial fall in company profitability during the period. Coupled with the squeeze on bank lending, the high cost of money and the increase in company taxation, this produced the liquidity problem which dominated company affairs in the late 1960s. Retrenchment and survival were principal preoccupations of most companies, whatever their size, and of almost all small and medium-sized companies. The difficult conditions accelerated the closing down of declining industries and hampered the establishment of new ones. The figures for company formations 1960–70 give a clear illustration of the slowing down in the creation of new businesses and the figures for company liquidations of the accelerated decline of existing ones.

TABLE NINE

	New businesses	*Liquidations*
1960	34,620	4,547
1961	33,997	5,025
1962	35,174	5,258
1963	42,535	5,542
1964	48,733	5,519
1965	36,681	7,136
1966	28,512	12,139
1967	31,597	8,943
1968	20,991	9,923
1969	25,451	9,046
1970	30,603	8,844

Personal bankruptcies showed a similar unwelcome increase. In employment terms this obviously meant a speeding up in the loss of jobs and loss of opportunities for new jobs.

A further useful indicator of the effect of the fall in consumer demand is the Capital Utilisation Index. Capital utilisation is defined in the *Bank of England Quarterly Bulletin* as the ratio of actual output to the potential output that could be produced from the existing capital stock assuming that adequate labour is available to operate plant and machinery.

TABLE TEN
CAPITAL UTILISATION INDEX
(1964 IV = 100)

	I	II	III	IV
1955	96·9	98·0	98·0	99·3
1956	97·0	94·5	93·7	93·2
1957	94·0	93·8	94·4	92·5
1958	92·6	90·8	89·8	89·3
1959	90·1	92·5	93·4	96·9
1960	98·7	98·3	97·8	97·0
1961	96·6	95·9	95·1	92·7
1962	90·9	93·3	93·2	90·6
1963	89·2	92·1	94·7	96·5
1964	98·0	97·5	98·0	100·0
1965	99·0	98·6	97·6	98·4
1966	98·6	97·2	97·2	93·3
1967	93·2	93·1	92·8	93·3
1968	93·9	94·5	95·5	95·8
1969	94·5	95·6	95·2	94·5
1970	94·0	91·8	92·6	93·1
1971	90·2*	91·1	90·6	

* Depressed by Ford strike.

The above index gives an indication of the spare capacity in our economy over the period 1955–71 and the graph opposite further illustrates the same point.

One notable feature is that although in 1958 and 1962 there were troughs, they were followed very rapidly by peaks. From the fourth quarter of 1966 we see a consistently mediocre and low level of capital utilisation. This must have had a cumulative effect on industrial confidence, and goes a long way to explaining the low rate of growth of fixed capital investment since 1966, and some way to explaining the dramatic fall in the number of employees since the first half of that year.

CAPITAL UTILISATION AND UNEMPLOYMENT

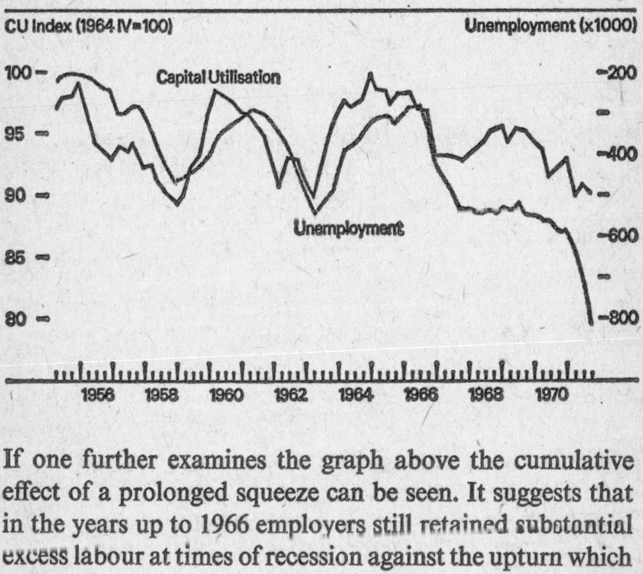

If one further examines the graph above the cumulative effect of a prolonged squeeze can be seen. It suggests that in the years up to 1966 employers still retained substantial excess labour at times of recession against the upturn which was assumed to be inevitable. In 1958 and 1963 recovery from recession was speedy and dramatic and unemployment never rose above 600,000. There was no such recovery from the decline of 1966 and it was the Government's intention that there should be none.

Lack of demand, leading as it did to substantial spare capacity in the economy over a very long period, undoubtedly played its part in creating unemployment. Even more significantly, it inflicted severe damage on industrial confidence and the restoration of that confidence is a principal obstacle in the way of making substantial reductions in the level of unemployment.

Perhaps the most important lesson to be learned is that if too much of one's economic effort is put into solving only one aspect of our economic problems, namely our external trade position, that over-emphasis will have to be paid for at some future date and will produce problems as significant as the one it is aiming to solve.

SHAKE-OUT

Nevertheless, there are other important reasons why a person can lose his job apart from lack of orders. A company may have many orders but it may have decided to instal a new piece of machinery which will do the work that was previously done by a number of people. Or the work can be organised in such a way that fewer people are needed to achieve the same result. Alternatively, a technological change may do away with tasks that previously were necessary. An example of this could be the development of cars which did not need servicing, so eliminating a major source of employment for garage mechanics.

If any one of these factors is the reason why a person loses his job, the stimulation of demand and more orders are not going to bring back that job for him.

If one looks first at the recent trends, the most obvious feature of the last decade in the pattern of employment has been the continuing reduction of the labour force in the traditionally labour-intensive industries. These are agriculture, mining, ship-building and textiles. In agriculture the numbers engaged have fallen from 968,000 in 1960 to 670,000 in 1970; in mining from 766,000 in 1960 to 410,000 in 1971; in ship building from 253,000 in 1960 to 190,000 in 1971; in textiles from 841,000 in 1960 to 612,000 in

1971. In these four areas alone, therefore, nearly a million jobs have ceased to exist during this period. Of these four areas, only in mining can lack of demand be accepted as a factor. In other cases in spite of the very substantial reduction in numbers employed, the output is now greater than it was ten years ago. Even in the case of miners, although the numbers employed have almost halved, the output this year is estimated (without the strike) still to have been 80 per cent of what it was in 1962.

A particularly clear example of the impact of new methods of working comes from the docks. In 1960 the number of registered dock workers was 72,000 and in 1970 this figure was reduced to 47,000, which is still considered by many to be considerably in excess of the numbers really required. At the same time the traffic handled has grown by approximately 20 per cent in volume. This reflects the impact of the two main developments in shipping: the special purpose bulk carrier, with high speed discharging equipment, and the container ship. Container ships represent one of the most extreme examples of reduction of employment opportunity. A 7,000-ton cargo ship of the old type would take on average 150 men ten days to unload. Now a container ship carrying a thousand 10-ton containers could be unloaded by fifteen men in one day. And so in theory where a hundred men were needed before, only one, plus the right equipment, is required.

From one point of view, this could be presented as the ultimate success in a campaign in which considerable management effort has been concentrated throughout industry to reduce the number of employees. This effort started with full Government support in the early 60s – or earlier – and was endorsed by the National Plan in 1965, because of the belief that this country's growth would be handicapped by a shortage of labour. Managements initially were slow to respond, but what stimulated them was the sharp increase in labour costs at a time of difficult trading conditions. The reduction of labour costs became essential for survival and there is no question that this has been an important factor in the rise of unemployment. It is worth recalling some words of William Beveridge's from a broadcast back in 1931 when he said that 'Many people are so determined not to believe that a good thing like high wages can cause a bad thing like unemployment, that they cheat themselves and they try to cheat others with every kind of false distinction and bad argument to the contrary.' Similarly, C. F. Pratten (in *Lloyds Bank Review*, January 1972) suggested that it is possible for a 5 per cent increase in wages to cause a 0·5 per cent fall in the labour force.

If our extreme example from shipping illustrates the way technology can reduce the employment opportunities for 'blue collar' workers, how is the position of 'white collar' workers affected? Later on this new feature of the current employment situation is discussed in more detail. At this stage it is interesting to note how the technology of management itself has affected 'white collar' employment. An example of what happened in one plant over the past twelve years illustrates this point.

Twelve years ago this plant, employing approximately 700 people and producing high quality products, was managed by one factory manager, assisted by one factory accountant and one chemist. (This plant was a production unit of a large group, so no sales management etc. was involved). The separate departments within the plant were managed by foremen who were directly responsible to the factory manager.

This rudimentary structure of management had served

very well when market conditions were favourable, but as competition increased it became clear that improvements were needed. At the same time the group was increasingly promoting new management techniques. The result of all this was that within six years the management of the plant had grown to one factory manager, one production manager, one technical manager, one production control manager, one works study manager, one quality control manager and the accountant, plus additional supporting staff. All these people made a useful contribution and many matters were dealt with much more thoroughly than might have been the case in the past.

The plant, however, did not make any more money! Indeed, when market conditions were difficult it made much less with the substantial overheads that it now carried. Market conditions became increasingly competitive and it proved very hard to get adequate prices for the company's products. The only way to improve the profitability of the plant was, therefore, to reduce costs and an obvious target were the overheads represented by certain of the 'white collar' activities. The situation now is that the plant is managed by a small, sophisticated management team, larger in number than that which originally existed twelve years ago but nothing like as large as that which was created in the mid-1960's.

The signs are that the experience of this plant is paralleled in many other companies.

Two factors that influence the level of unemployment are the rate at which old jobs disappear and the rate at which new opportunities occur. There is considerable evidence, therefore, that the real change in most recent years is that while old jobs have continued to disappear, more sophisticated management techniques have reduced or eliminated the growth of employment that would otherwise have occurred in many of the newer industries.

Banking is one example of this. There has been growth in the number of accounts handled and also in the range of services provided, but the impact of the computer, together with mergers, has stabilised the numbers employed and prevented the increase that might otherwise have been expected to occur.

On the service side, similarly, there is the impact of super-markets on the number engaged in retail trading. The statistics conceal the position as they show numbers employed and the main casualty from the super-markets has been a host of small self-employed shopkeepers. The growth of super-markets and the concentration of retail outlets into fewer hands has had a further impact on the selling staffs required by a considerable number of companies. The *caravanserai* of commercial travellers that was a recognised feature of British life has virtually ceased to exist and supplies to the shops in the High Streets are increasingly ordered from central points.

Clearly, areas have been identified where a measure of shake-out has certainly occurred. This does not, however, prove that it is a predominant factor in the recent sharp increase and until recently the official Department of Employment view still seemed to discount it in its analysis of the current situation. However, as we have seen, the Prime Minister in his speech on 24th January laid particular stress on this factor and, indeed, referred to the 'massive shake-out' of labour that had occurred. Support for this new emphasis on the significance of shake-out comes from the recently completed CBI survey of manufacturing industry. This showed that in the period from September 1971 to January 1972, on their weighted-average sample system, twice as many companies had increased output as those that had reduced it. During that same time nearly four times as many companies had reduced their numbers employed as had increased them. Further evidence from this survey shows that while shake-out has not yet finished, it is reducing considerably, and on the same basis of figures, from January to May in 1972, while 49 per cent expect output to increase as against 13 per cent who expect it to decrease, only 27 per cent expect their numbers employed to be lower, and indeed 16 per cent of the remainder actually expected to take on more.

In the search for further understanding of the causes behind the recent high level of redundancies a small survey was conducted of firms which declared more than fifty redundancies in the month of October 1971.

At the time of going to press thirty-three replies have been received. This is obviously a very small sample and could not be grounds for any major conclusions but the findings nevertheless do provide some interesting pointers. The particular object of the questionnaire was to establish the cause of the redundancies and to establish in how many cases, if lack of sales was the reason for the redundancies, revival of sales would lead to re-employment. In eight companies, however, which involved 1,388 jobs the companies had closed down and so there was no question of re-employment. Seven further companies, which had sacked 652 people between them, did blame the reductions on lack of sales and might re-employ if sales recovered. A further eleven companies who had dismissed 4,573 did not anticipate that a sales recovery would lead to any re-employment. A significant theme running through a number of these replies was that in the majority of cases the firms were of medium size with approximately 850 employees and that they were all reducing by approximately 150 people, although expecting 10–20 per cent increase in sales in the coming year.

The simplest judgement on the majority of these firms was that they were reorganising with the effect of achieving a 10 per cent increase in sales with a 10 per cent reduction in numbers employed. This small survey certainly lent force to the view that the prolonged squeeze on demand triggered off redundancies and slowed down the rate of investment. It also suggested that rocketing costs and shake-out accelerated the process and that only a substantial and sustained increase in demand and the rate of growth will compensate for the present rate of shake-out. And while this sample *proves* nothing, the story it tells is probably being repeated in many other cases.

CHAPTER THREE

The productivity pattern

THE LAST CHAPTER sought to illuminate the extent to which unemployment is being caused by shake-out, as opposed to lack of demand. This chapter will take this further with a varied series of examples, ending with a look at one region. They should perhaps be prefaced with the comment that it is difficult to separate technological from managerial or shake-out factors, certainly as far as the official statistics are concerned. Indeed, even structural unemployment – in the sense of unemployment produced by changes in the structure of industry, notably the run-down of the older industries like coal-mining or cotton manufacture – is not easily separated from other forms of unemployment, although nobody would dispute its significance.

In the cases that follow, therefore, the exact classification of unemployment may sometimes be hazy. Nevertheless, they have an important story to tell, in that they show what is happening to employment in certain specific industries.

TEXTILES, HOSIERY AND CLOTHING

As a generally labour-intensive industry, the textile, hosiery and clothing industry makes a valuable study. Because of its low level of capital intensity it is prone to violent swings between over and under capacity, and within these to seasonal fluctuations. A further factor at the present time is the increasing threat from and effect of low labour-cost imported goods.

Because of the size of the industry it has been necessary

to be selective.. The conclusions from this rather detailed case material which follows are summarised on page 37.

(*a*) *Courtaulds*

Relevant information for the large and diverse Courtaulds Group of companies drawn from the two reports for 31st March 1970 and 1971 is given below:

TABLE ELEVEN

	1969–70	*1970–71*
Total sales (000£)	626,546	659,583
Sales from UK manuf. (000£)	482,217	516,878
UK employees	137,819	136,331
Total UK remuneration (000£)	132,903	149,461
Turnover per employee (£s)	3,500	3,800

Employing over 100,000 people in the UK alone the group, apart from some interests in packaging and paint, is engaged mainly in the textile industry. Its scope ranges from man-made fibre production and the related chemicals manufacture through most of the vertical processes associated with yarn, fabric and garment manufacture to textile wholesaling.

The above figures show an increase in turnover per employee of 8½ per cent whilst the pressure on costs is partly illustrated by a 12½ per cent rise in total remuneration. Indeed, the 1970/71 report states that whilst wages, materials and other costs rose by well over £40m, 'prices overall were unchanged'; which indicates a labour productivity gain of the same 8½ per cent.

There is every reason to suppose that similar pressures on costs have continued into the current year and that a further reduction in employees has taken place.

This group is a perfect illustration of the pressures under which management has been to contain and/or cut costs.

In addition, it has been subject to intense competition from low labour-cost imports and in some cases from over-capacity which has resulted in the overall price stability referred to in the 1970/71 report.

The company has indulged in very big investment over the past few years. Its announced policy of lower investment over the immediate future is probably justified in the light of this but there is no question but that cash flow has been a matter of considerable concern to the management at times during the period under review.

With a continuing drive for and expectation of further increases in labour productivity there are no grounds for anticipating any significant rise in numbers employed over the next year or two.

(b) Lancashire textile industry

Figures obtained from the *Quarterly Statistical Review* (Winter 1971/1972) give the following general picture:

TABLE TWELVE

	1969	*1970*	*1970*		*1971*	
			3rd Qtr.	*4th Qtr.*	*3rd Qtr.*	*Oct (prov.)*
Index of textile prodn (CSO) 1963 = 100	123·6	124·0	120·8	125·9	126·3	127·0
Daily rate of prodn.						
Single yarn - mn lb.	2·16	2·18	2·20	2·18	1·92	1·99
Woven cloth - mn yards	5·38	5·09	4·94	4·96	4·75	4·79
Employment – '000						
Spinning/Doubling	46·27	45·01	45·20	44·47	39·26	37·71
Weaving	46·25	43·03	42·54	41·37	38·25	37·88
Finishing	22·93	21·56	21·48	20·99	20·27	20·32
Total	115·45	109·60	109·22	106·83	97·78	95·91

For comparison and because of the expansion in fabric knitting, the following table is inserted here:

TABLE THIRTEEN
AVERAGE NUMBER OF EMPLOYEES

	1967 (*000s*)	*1968* (*000s*)	*1969* (*000s*)	*1970* (*000s*)
Warp knitting	7·61	8·81	9·67	9·23
Weft knitting (incl. fabric)	129·38	127·95	132·95	127·50

A study of cotton spinning shows the following:

TABLE FOURTEEN

	Dec. 64	*Oct. 71*	*% change*
Employees	47,520	27,740	minus 41
Weekly prodn.mn. lb.	10·8	8·4	minus 22

This sector has been severely hit by foreign imports accounting for an over 20 per cent contraction in production. On the other hand labour productivity overall has increased in the period by 33 per cent.

What is most significant, though, is that one major part of this industry, covering the actual ring spinning process and all preparation for it, has in contrast to the rest of the trade recently carried out a massive re-organisation programme. It can be shown that if the rest of the industry were to modernise to the standard already achieved by that more efficient section there would be further redundancies of over 4,000 jobs out of the present total of approximately 28,000.

Nor is the industry standing still technologically. For instance, spinning processes have already been developed and are in limited use which increase productivity by 100 per cent, although total replacement of conventional techniques is not expected due to different characteristics in the product.

Further redundancies in textiles would have occurred if the Government had not announced its continuation of quotas on cotton for 1972. It is doubtful, though, whether much of the unmodernised section of the industry can find the amount of cash necessary for the investment required, and further loss of jobs, moderated by an up-turn in business activity, are inevitable. The modernised section expects a higher production level in 1972 to be balanced by further improvements in labour productivity so that the employment prospects remain constant.

(c) *Hosiery – stockings and tights*

In this case imports have been of less significance but over-capacity combined with technical progress have been the vital factors. Prices have dropped sharply over the past two or three years.

Four examples of companies engaged in a mixture of brand, bulk and contract selling of tights and stockings have been studied specially. These companies, employing between them over 2,200 people, have modern plant and progressive production and management techniques.

Taking figures available for the end of 1971 it is shown that in these companies production has increased by 11 per cent p.a. over the previous two years whilst employees have decreased by 11½ per cent p.a. Labour productivity has risen by approximately 30 per cent p.a.

A significant fact is that an increase in employees of 6 per cent is expected for 1972 to give a 16 per cent increase in production but the numbers employed will still be considerably less than in 1969. The rise in productivity, although lower than the previous average, will be at a still healthy 10 per cent. It should be added that the product mix has changed, i.e. increasingly more tights have been manufactured, so that the above production and productivity figures are in fact understated.

(*d*) *Hosiery – knitwear*

Incomplete data from four sample companies, with total employment of about 12,000 people indicates a gradual rise in employment of about 5 per cent p.a. over the last three years, to give an additional 12 per cent annual turnover. The increased sales value per employee of 7 per cent p.a. is estimated to derive from increased productivity (2 per cent) and higher prices (5 per cent).

(*e*) *The clothing industry*

(Including outerwear, sleepwear, men's wear, children's wear etc., but not hosiery and knitwear).

The latest NEDC statistical bulletin for Great Britain covering up to the end of 1971 shows the change in employment in this sector since 1963. ('000 approx).

TABLE FIFTEEN

	1963	*1969*	*1970*	*1971*
Males	95	86	81	81
Females	346	315	300	302
TOTAL	441	401	381	383

The downward trend at 5 per cent in 1969–70 was arrested in 1970–71. Men's and women's earnings rose by 12 per cent to 12½ per cent in the one year from 1969 to 1970 and by 8½ and 10 per cent in 1971 whilst productivity increases of about 8 per cent and 5 per cent respectively were achieved in the two years.

Of individual companies studied a striking example was found of one judged to be most efficiently managed and also satisfactorily profitable. Up to September 1971 this company had cut its work force by 8 per cent p.a. over the preceding two years, and had increased sales by 11 per cent and turnover per employee by 23 per cent p.a. Adjusted for price increases, the productivity increase might be approximately 15 per cent p.a.

It is difficult to calculate the effect on the industry's costs of equal pay for women. In most cases jobs are separate but average earnings in 1970 at £24·12 for men and £13·23 for women illustrate the differentials which exist.

Imports at an estimated £125m. (NEDC) in 1971 will have increased by about 50 per cent in the last two years and pose a serious threat to employment. On the other hand, the stabilisation of employment in the clothing industry in 1971 is encouraging and it is reasonable to expect a continuing and positive response to demand.

However a shake-out has occurred in this sector largely due to managements' attitude to wasteful labour and better utilisation, rather than to technological change. There is little reason for this attitude to be relaxed. Contrarily, there is very considerable scope for increases in labour productivity through better work handling.

Conclusions

Because the textile, hosiery and clothing industry is labour-intensive, managements have responded strongly to wage and salary increases by achieving at least average but generally higher than average labour productivity gains.

The shake-out is due to a combination of the effects of technological change and of managements' attitude to surplus labour and to labour utilisation. It is possible to point to the relative importance of these two factors in different sectors, but difficult to quantify them.

In Lancashire, where productivity increases have been lower, there is scope for major modernisation on the lines of the leading firms, which would result in further redundancies.

In clothing and hosiery, employment will respond to consumer demand (again because of labour-intensity) and indeed this is already occurring in clothing. On the other hand, managements' critical attitude to labour utilisation is not likely to change and there is a massive potential for further productivity increases through improved work handling and flow, with comparatively low capital expenditure.

Because of its nature, the industry not unnaturally claims protection from imports from low labour-cost countries.

Generally there seems little expectation of increase in numbers employed over the next year or two, with the effects of growth being counter-balanced by productivity gains.

ENGINEERING

Our next example comes from engineering. It serves both to show productivity trends, and to introduce some regional complications in the picture. The tables below show the trend of employment output and earnings in two British companies over the period from 1967 to 1971.

TABLE SIXTEEN

COMPANY A

	Midlands plant		**Scottish plant**	
Year	*Av. hourly earnings*	*Output per man hour*	*Av. hourly earnings*	*Output per man hour*
1967	100 (@ 634p)	100	100 (@ 651p)	100
1968	106	111	113	97·3
1969	113	117	123	106
1970	130	126	143	110
1971	144	134	149	114

The following deductions may be made from the figures:

(i) Company A has had poor experience in Scotland with its factory built to obtain benefits of a development area location.

(ii) Wages were higher in 1967 in the Scottish plant than in the Midlands plant and over the five-year period they rose at a faster rate.

(iii) Output per man hour failed in both plants to keep pace with the rise in average hourly earnings. In the Scottish plant the experience was very much worse than in the Midlands although capital investment was comparable in both locations.

(iv) It is apparent that in this example, the output/earnings ratio of the Scottish plant has worsened relative to the Midlands year by year.

TABLE SEVENTEEN

COMPANY B

Year	*Total number of employees*	*Total number of shopfloor employees – direct labour*	*Sales value in £ per employee*	*Value of production i.e. sales plus adjusted stock movement in £ per shopfloor employee – direct*
1969	3,021	1,600	5,600	7,000
1970	3,334	1,735	5,200	9,400
1971	3,076	1,506	6,200	11,000

The following deductions may be made from the figures:

(i) Although the total number of employees has remained fairly static over three years, the sales value per employee has risen by 17 per cent.

(ii) The total number of shopfloor employees on direct wages fell by 6 per cent and there was a massive rise of output per shopfloor employee of 57 per cent involving a rise from £7,000 per employee to £11,000.

(iii) Capital expenditure on machinery over the preceding years amounted to about £500 per shopfloor employee each year and this bore fruit in the larger output per man.

(iv) It would appear that the next major area where efficiency must be increased in Company B is in general, administrative and selling expenses.

Both companies are in the engineering industry. Company A has two large plants in the Midlands and Scotland, while Company B has seven smaller plants in the Midlands and London. The two companies A and B are not strictly comparable but one or two points emerge from them:

(i) The rise in output per man has been considerable, particularly on the shopfloor and in the medium-sized rather than large plants.

(ii) The development area location may be associated with steadily declining efficiency.

(iii) The Midlands seems the most desirable location for manufacturing, in spite of the grants available in development areas.

We shall return to regional policy later in this pamphlet, but these examples help to illustrate the sort of substantial, if uneven, productivity increases which are taking place in industry to-day.

A SERVICE INDUSTRY: ADVERTISING

The reduction of labour forces in recent years has not taken place in manufacturing industry alone. Service industries also have been compelled to trim their staffs. Advertising agencies provide an example of what has been happening.

In 1966 there were 20,000 people employed by member agencies of the Institute of Practitioners in Advertising, which between them place some 70 per cent of all advertis-

TABLE EIGHTEEN

1966	20,000	1969	17,200
1967	18,600	1970	17,200
1968	17,900	1971	15,600

ing in the United Kingdom. Since 1966 the numbers employed have fallen as shown in Table Eighteen.

Meanwhile, turnover has increased from £355m. in 1966 to £406m. in 1970, and turnover per person employed from £18,000 in 1966 to £23,500 in 1970.

In advertising agencies, unlike many areas of manufacturing industry, it has not been the impact of new machines but the trend of profits and the pressure of rising costs that has led to the reduction of jobs. Profits as a percentage of agency income have fallen as follows:

TABLE NINETEEN

1960	19·2%	1968	12·0%
1966	11·6%	1969	11·2%
1967	11·0%	1970	9·3%

During the same period total costs have been rising and agencies have been compelled to restrict the share of costs that is accountable to the payroll. As a result fewer people have been employed, though more money has been paid to those retained. In 1967 £32m. was paid for 18,600 people; in 1968 £33½m. for 17,900 people and in 1969 £35½m. for 17,200.

In advertising, as elsewhere, mergers and amalgamations have been a consequence of the search for better profits. In 1966 100 out of 276 IPA agencies were linked within groups of two or more. By 1970 more than 150 agencies were linked with one or more others, and it would be surprising if the result had not been some further reduction in manpower.

There are now signs of a recovery in the rate of growth of expenditure on advertising. Even so, it is unlikely that this will lead to a comparable rise in the numbers employed. One reason for this caution is that the productivity figures for British agencies still lag behind those for American agencies, and indeed for a number of countries on the continent of Europe.

A second reason emerges from the recent experience of the leading agency in Britain, the J. Walter Thompson Company. There substantial increases in billings during the past five years have been absorbed without any comparable increase in staff. The figures are as follows:

TABLE TWENTY

	Billing	*Average staff numbers*
1966	£20·9 m.	903
1967	£22·4 m.	917
1968	£22·7 m.	888
1969	£25·3 m.	905
1970	£28·9 m.	929
1971	£30·6 m.	934

The lessons to be learned from the last five years appear clear enough. Agencies have been exerting themselves to control their payroll costs, which account for 56 per cent of their total costs, in the face of rising costs elsewhere. These efforts are likely to continue and it would be unwise to predict any major increase in the numbers of people they will employ.

THE SOUTH-WEST

We conclude this chapter with a brief look at what has been happening in a region, as opposed to an industry. The South-West includes such divergent areas as Severnside, where there is a considerable amount of manufacturing industry, and Devon and Cornwall where the economy is primarily dependent on tourism and agriculture. The shift in employment from one sector of the economy to another in the South-West over the nine years from 1961 to 1970 has been as follows:

TABLE TWENTY-ONE

EMPLOYEES IN EMPLOYMENT

	1961	*1970*
Agriculture	58,500	35,580
Extractive	20,632	15,659
Manufacturing	383,152	418,063
Construction	100,609	85,908
Services	607,126	662,975
Total	1,170,019	1,218,185

During the same period the number unemployed has grown substantially:

TOTAL WHOLLY UNEMPLOYED

1961 *(June)*	*1970* *(June)*	*%change*
11,659	34,290	+200

The following deductions may be made from the figures:

(i) Although the number of jobs available has increased it has been insufficient to prevent a substantial rise in the number of unemployed.

(ii) The number employed in services has risen but it has been insufficient to cover the fall of employment in agriculture, extraction and construction.

(iii) Assuming a static population in the South-West in the 1970s it is unlikely that further rises in the services sector will be able to offset any decline in manufacturing and other employment.

Comparable figures for the old South-West Development area (West, North and Central Cornwall plus North Devon) were as follows:

TABLE TWENTY-TWO

NUMBER OF EMPLOYEES IN EMPLOYMENT

	1961	*1971*
Agriculture	11,570	5,754
Extraction	7,917	7,766
Manufacturing	18,026	29,124
Construction	9,755	9,663
Services	74,392	75,267
Total	121,660	127,644

During the same period the number of unemployed has grown substantially:

TOTAL WHOLLY UNEMPLOYED

1961 *(June)*	*1970* *(June)*	*% change*
1,947	4,975	150

The following deductions may be made from the figures:

(i) Development area incentives have been successful in increasing the number of jobs available in the area in the summer (June) month.

(ii) The increase in employment in services in an area in which tourism is the major industry has been relatively small.

(iii) The rise of employment in manufacturing and services has been inadequate to offset the fall in other sectors, hence there has been a substantial rise in unemployment.

(iv) The comparable figures for the December/January months are not available but unemployment is normally about three times the June figures at this time of year. This means that the new jobs created (about 6,000) have fallen considerably behind the increase in the number unemployed in the winter of say, 13,000 men and women.

CHAPTER FOUR

White collar unemployment

THE LEAST UNDERSTOOD aspect of the present unemployment situation is the position of white collar workers. Although the monthly figures published by the Department of Employment are broken down in a variety of ways, they do not tell us how many executives, managers and office staff are now without jobs. The only guide, apart from incomplete and sometimes rather impressionistic research studies, is the rough rule of thumb that there is probably one for every ten people from the shop floor. This means a total of over 90,000 which includes men (and some women) with salaries ranging from £1,500 to £25,000 a year.

The time when a white collar job meant security, and the extent of that security increased the higher you rose up the management ladder, has gone. Indeed, it looks as if the causes of the large number of white collar redundancies arise from fundamental changes in the position of British industry and in its management attitudes. Consequently, the problem cannot be expected to disappear when the pace of economic growth accelerates, nor to diminish in line with the decline that will no doubt take place in the over-all unemployment statistics.

The great majority of the white collar unemployed are from the lower reaches of management and the ranks of the clerical and non-professional staff. In general, these are people earning between £1,500 a year and £2,800 plus car. But there are also significant numbers who have been accustomed to earning very much more. All the circumstantial evidence suggests that there is a record number of directors and top executives accustomed to earning upwards of £5,000 a year looking for work.

Whatever the difference in their background, the white collar unemployed have one thing in common. They have not been sacked in response to a passing change in the economic climate or in their former companies' order book in order to be taken back later. Their jobs have frequently been eliminated as part of a series of conscious and deliberate moves designed to achieve a once-and-for-all reduction in costs. They cannot expect to return to their old jobs and, as much of industry has been subjected to the same pressures, they will probably find it very difficult to secure a similar position elsewhere.

The problem can be seen at its most stark at the lower end of the income scale. It is clear that there the most far-reaching cost-cutting can be achieved. Companies are naturally loathe to reveal their activities in this field. But the experience of one leading concern in a technically advanced industry, which has reduced the total number employed in its clerical, non-professional staff, and junior management grades, from 2,000 in 1968 to about 1,500 now, is not untypical. In many companies the percentage is often higher.

The jobs these men used to do have frequently disappeared altogether. The arrival of computers has led to a substantial drop in the number of staff who used to handle the receipt and despatch of invoices and bills. This applies particularly in the service industries and activities such as insurance. The spread of numerically-controlled machine tools has cut down the need for white collar supervision as well as needing fewer men on the shop floor to secure higher output. In chemicals, oil, and other process industries, automation means fewer jobs for those who used to act as controllers.

The desire to reduce costs by cutting staff overheads has been stimulated in part by the rash of mergers and take-overs that has characterised British industry in recent years. Whole industries, such as motors, electrical engineering and steel, have been completely reorganised. Notwithstanding the opposition of the trade unions, this has led to redundancies among factory workers, sometimes on a dramatic scale. Managers have tended to be much harder hit.

Seniority and position are no protection in these circumstances. When a merger or take-over occurs, it is always necessary to ensure that duplication should be avoided. When two companies are in the same field, this can mean a large-scale loss of jobs. But even where they are supposedly complementary to each other, there is plenty of scope for cost reduction in such service functions as advertising, personnel, planning and administration. At the highest levels where the number of positions is fewest, the competition in jobs is most intense and the wastage rate frequently highest in terms of percentages, though not numbers.

The concentration of industry adds enormously to a man's problems in finding alternative employment, whether he comes from the top or the bottom. Electrical engineering provides a case in point. Where once there were three giants, now there is only one. The man who loses his job in one of the successive mergers finds that the firm which sacked him has become the principal if not the sole employer of people with his skills.

Quite apart from take-overs, there are signs that British industry is becoming more ruthless in its attitude towards managers and other white collar staff. The traditional reluctance to sack began to break down during the 1960s when the squeeze on company profits intensified. The more ruthless approach was given further encouragement by the growing determination of governments of both parties to attack restrictive trade practices of every sort. Another important factor has been the mounting competition, both from imports and foreign-owned companies operating in this country. Under a Conservative Government profits should improve during the 1970s, but the other factors should continue to apply, and companies will be forced to ensure that their salaries bill is kept tightly under control. The faster the level of salaries rises, the more determined will employers become to keep their companies as lean as possible.

The growth of a more ruthless attitude is accompanied by the application of more demanding standards over an ever-widening area of managerial and executive activity. This is partly because of the spread of business education and of magazines and periodicals dealing with business subjects. But these phenomena owe their popularity to a desire to emulate the performance of the most successful concerns. These concerns themselves are extending their operations across frontiers, while domestic companies are realising that the only way to increase profits is to adopt the most up-to-date techniques.

Thus the standards developed by multinational companies in their most competitive markets are becoming those that everyone must live by. This in turn means that it is necessary for managers and executives to prove that they have mastered the intricacies of the latest techniques in their particular fields. They must also expect to be judged by more clearly defined and objective criteria than in the past. The penalty for failure is likely to be severe.

From a national economic point of view, this trend has several advantages. It represents an attempt by British industry to become as efficient and competitive as its principal foreign rivals. It also means that able and ambitious younger men should be able to get fast promotion and better opportunities instead of being held back in frustration until their elders retire.

But the social costs must be counted. It is the duty of the Government to ensure that the rights and interests of individuals are respected. The worst sufferers from the new industrial attitudes tend to be men over forty, who have often spent a working lifetime within a single industry or professional occupation, and sometimes with a single firm. When they lose their jobs they are unfitted for any alternative employments, and psychologically affected as well.

The first priority is to ensure that far more comprehensive statistics are collected. It is necessary to have more detailed information about who is out of work and why before the problem can be satisfactorily tackled.

There is, too, an urgent need for a larger and more effective service for bringing the white collar unemployed into contact with prospective employers. The Government's recent decision to improve the Professional and Executive Register is a useful first step. But the limitations on the resources that can be made available to it mean that much will have to depend on services run by private enterprise and non-Governmental bodies. These should be helped where possible.

Fear of the sack has done more than anything else over the last few years to encourage white collar workers to join trade unions. Men who would never have done so in order to increase their salaries have decided, often regretfully, that this is the best way to secure reasonable contracts of employment. They realise that a contract will not guarantee them a job, but they need the protection it provides, in the sense of guaranteeing reasonable notice and the provision of reasonable financial terms.

This is an area that should engage the attention of Government. Although trade unions have a part to play it is essential that a framework should be established that ensures a basic set of standards for all white collar workers, whether or not they are members of a trade union. White collar workers, especially those over forty, have special interests that are not the same as the mass of industrial workers. This does not mean that they should be accorded special privileges, but it does mean that they should receive the protection they require.

In the long-term there will no doubt be changes in the pattern of the white-collar worker's professional life. As industry becomes more technical and change more rapid, so experience will be set at a discount and a premium put on adaptability. This will make it desirable to promote young men and women more quickly and to retire older people earlier. But this does not provide an answer to the short-term problem. Moreover, it must not be thought that early retirement is a panacea. If people are not to feel that they have been thrown on a scrapheap when they give up their professional careers at a relatively early age, they must prepare very carefully for their life in retirement. In so doing they will require a good deal of external help from their employers and probably from the State. Eventually early retirement may enable people to lead fuller and happier lives than at present. If, however, they are forced to retire earlier than they would wish, without proper preparation or financial provision, they will face disaster.

CHAPTER FIVE

Multinational companies

ONE OF THE COMPLICATING factors in any assessment of future unemployment is the existence of multinational companies. There is no doubt that they will play an important part in determining the level of employment in Britain during the 1970s and beyond.

The definition of such a company is that it simultaneously carries on the various aspects of its business in several different countries. This gives it far more flexibility than a purely national company. A national concern must plan its investments in new plant and equipment, and the extent of its export effort, in the context of the economic prospects of the country in which it is situated. The multinational company, by contrast, can choose between the various countries where its subsidiaries operate. Britain must get its fair share when these choices are made.

Multinational companies have become the characteristic industrial organisation of the age. To an increasing extent, they dominate the most vital, the largest, the most pervasive, and often the fastest growing industries. General Motors and Ford in cars, Shell and Esso in oil, IBM in computers, Unilever and Procter and Gamble in detergents, Kodak in photographic materials, Philips in electrical products, Alcan and Rio Tinto Zinc in metals, and Olivetti in typewriters, are just a few of the most obvious examples. While national concerns predominate in the old declining industries like coal and shipbuilding, the multinationals are taking over the new commanding heights.

Some are British owned, others American or Canadian,

and a number come from the Continent. But whatever their country of origin, they build their plants and sell their products all over the world. When they plan their strategies they do so on an international scale.

In the last few years Britain has been losing out when these companies decide where to concentrate their best efforts. Ford and General Motors (which produces Vauxhalls in this country and Opels on the continent) provide a classic illustration of what has been happening. Both have their principal European subsidiaries in Britain and Germany, and between 1959 and 1968 they increased the net fixed assets of their German subsidiaries four times as fast as their British.

In the expanding economies of the post-war western world there is no question of prosperous multinational companies closing down vast plants, like Ford's at Dagenham, and moving them to another country. The process is more subtle. A contemporary industrial plant needs to be constantly modernised and expanded if it is to achieve the maximum possible growth available to it within the context of the performance of its owner and industry. Ford and General Motors have invested enormously in this country: indeed, they have done better than many national concerns. The crucial point, however, is that they have expanded their operations more rapidly elsewhere. In real terms we have dropped behind. Britain has had the same experience with some other industries as well.

Dropping behind is bad enough. It is much worse when plants less efficient than those owned by Ford and General Motors sack some of their employees or close down altogether. Multinational companies can run into difficulties and find themselves forced to do this just like any other company. No government can guard against business failures or setbacks, especially with companies that function across frontiers. But when a company is looking for ways to retrench its least profitable plants, those in countries where the economic outlook is least promising will be the first to suffer.

The great majority of companies in this country are not, of course, multinational. In terms of their share of manufacturing investment and of labour employed, the multinationals can be made to appear relatively insignificant, although the Government has no reliable figures on either point. Their importance in the economy derives from one fact that their operations are the key to the prosperity of many other companies.

When Shell, for instance, announces a multi-million pound addition to its chemical plants, or Alcan builds a £40m. plus aluminium smelter, orders flow throughout the economy. Similarly, the level of output at Ford's determines the order books and so the number of jobs available at a host of sub-contractors.

The scope of multinational business will increase substantially during the 1970s. Its growth so far owes much to the reduction of tariffs and to the gradual removal of non-tariff barriers to trade in the 1960s. With the expansion of the Common Market and the attempts that are likely to be made to establish a new economic relationship between the Common Market, North America and Japan, the trend will accelerate. More large companies will extend their foreign operations, and many small ones will follow. Some will do so because of the opportunities to secure economies of scale and greater flexibility, and others because it will be the only way to provide a comprehensive service to their industrial customers.

By joining the Common Market Britain puts itself into a position to compete with the other European countries on equal terms for new investment. Our exclusion during the

1960s was one reason why we attracted less investment than we would have liked from multinational companies, both British and foreign-owned. This was partly because of our poor economic growth record compared with those of our neighbours, and partly because of the relatively small size of our market. In many industries the optimum size of new plants has become very large. Consequently they need large domestic markets in which to sell. Supplying a small market and relying on exports for a high proportion of total sales is a far more risky and less satisfactory arrangement than the opportunity to sell most of the output in a large market, with exports as a useful addition.

However, Britain still has a number of disadvantages. Of these, the international reputation of our labour relations is amongst the most important.

The British record in this respect is not as bad in terms of days lost as is sometimes thought. But the unpredictability of labour relations here, and the frequency of wild-cat strikes that disrupt whole areas of industry, are serious disadvantages. They are particularly relevant in multinational business operations, since the activities of a company's plants in different countries are integrated with each other. Thus, a stoppage in Britain can lead to production lines being brought to a halt and men being laid off in several other countries.

The labour situation should improve following the passage of the Industrial Relations Act, but it will be some time before multinational managers recognise this. Like other human beings, they are not free from prejudice, and their doubts over Britain's labour relations may prove difficult to dispel.

Another British disadvantage is inflation. This disease is to be found in all industrial countries. But in Britain it has been worse than most. Accountants are only just beginning to appreciate the full impact inflation can have on a company's real financial position. But already it is clear that the implications, so far as the differences between historic and replacement costs, the value of stocks, the assessment of rates of return, and other matters are concerned, will be profound.

Finally, Britain has an appalling record of industrial profits. As a proportion of the total domestic income they have fallen from 15 per cent in 1964 to 10·1 per cent in 1970 and 9·6 per cent in the first quarter of 1971. Not surprisingly, rates of return on investments in the EEC countries have tended to be significantly better than those in Britain. On both the inflation and the company profits fronts the situation has improved a good deal in recent months. Government policies are designed to ensure that this continues. But comparisons with the past are less important than those with other countries and, again, doubts will be difficult to dispel.

The growth of multinational companies has brought problems as well as opportunities in its train. Their ability to shift financial resources and the emphasis of their operations across frontiers, and the fact that governments sometimes compete for their investments almost like suitors for a bride's hand, have deeply worrying implications. There is an urgent need for governments to create a more satisfactory framework for dealing with these problems. But this does not alter the necessity to ensure that Britain secures its fair share of the economic and industrial benefits provided by the multinationals.

This country starts with several advantages. Our political system is stable and our capital markets second to none. English is the international business language and our labour force is technically skilled and accustomed to the needs and requirements of modern industrial life. Because of the high level of unemployment, labour is more freely available than on the continent, and within the development areas there is plenty of scope for building large new industrial units and expanding existing ones. If the weaknesses of poor labour relations, inflation and declining profit margins can be eradicated, we should be well placed to gain from the growth of multinational business operations – and hence to hold down unemployment.

PART TWO

SOME ANSWERS

CHAPTER SIX

Creating new jobs

IN CHAPTER TWO, we examined the balance between lack of demand and shake-out in creating the present unemployment. This chapter opens the second part of this pamphlet – on remedies – by evaluating the extent to which stepped-up demand may be expected to produce new jobs, and the degree to which we need to search for new areas of employment.

Professor Harry Johnson recently remarked 'if you think you can go round fixing up one thing at a time, you are kidding us and yourself as well.'

During the period 1966–70, the whole of the Labour Government's economic policy placed its emphasis on cutting back on consumer demand and therefore producing a switch of resources and an improvement in our external position. Until that period industry had learned to expect that a recession would be short-term and would be followed by quick recovery and a boom period, albeit a short one. Since 1966, industry has had substantial spare capacity and now views signs of recovery with great scepticism.

The danger in the present situation is that the Government, which has already reflated to an extent which most economists a year ago would have considered satisfactory, now finds itself being urged to take huge further reflationary steps.

What industry needs is not a spectacular one-off boost to demand but the prospect of steady and continuing growth. Over-reaction to the present low level of demand could give rise to balance of payments problems and we could find ourselves back on the old stop-go merry-go-round.

The Conservative Government has already created a much more favourable climate for industry to work in than has existed for many years. Money is available, interest rates are low, company taxation has been reduced. Company profitability is improving and companies are far more liquid than they have been for many years. What is holding industrial investment back is spare capacity and scepticism about whether the growth in consumer demand is temporary. After twenty-one quarters of operating below capacity, industry will need more than one or two quarters of improved demand before it believes the evidence of its own eyes. Over-reaction at the moment could well destroy and not create confidence.

Even if confidence does begin to return there will be a considerable time lag before growth reflects itself in a

CAPITAL UTILISATION AND VACANCIES

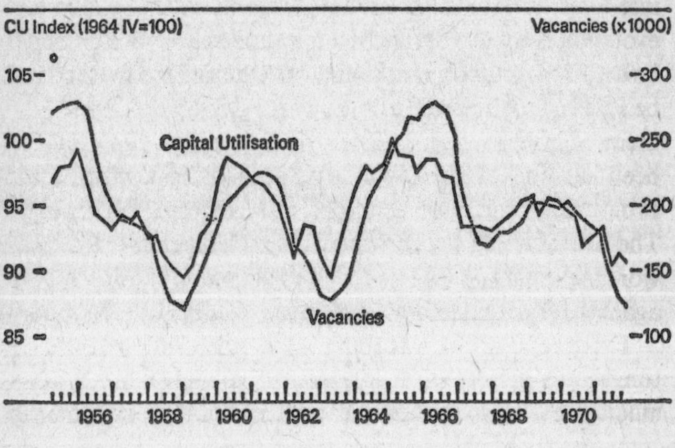

worthwhile reduction in the unemployment figures. The graph above showing the comparison between capital utilisation and vacancies illustrates this point quite well. Vacancies increase approximately one year later than the peak of capital utilisation. The reason is that employers tend to introduce overtime and shift work rather than increase their labour force in the early stages of recovery.

Measures to increase demand, then, are unlikely to absorb more than a proportion of our present unemployment. If that is so, it is important to see how new jobs can be stimulated other than by expansion of demand. But first we need so far as possible to make intelligent forecasts of employment levels in the future. We are able to make reasonably accurate forecasts of job reductions. We need to match this with the best possible forecasts of new job opportunities.

Work on this is being done in many countries, but there is not yet much evidence of any great advance in this field. It would certainly appear that Germany is well ahead of Britain and has two institutes already working in this field. While there has been criticism that the work done by these institutes is largely academic, it is said that plans are evolving by which 19,000,000 new job opportunities might be created by 1980 to replace those which it is expected will be lost through new methods of working. In this country there is little evidence as yet of how much progress has been made either by the Department of Employment and Productivity or now the Office of Manpower Economics. The Science Policy Unit of Sussex University has been working on this problem for the engineering industry, but again little is known of its progress.

The problem of identifying the potential job opportunities from new technology can be appreciated if one studies the chart on page 63, which originally appeared in

Science Journal, and was included in an issue of *Long Range Planning* in 1969. Many of the items obviously may have very considerable impact on the whole question of population and employment – for example, the possibility of extending life span by 50 years, or the breeding of intelligent animals for low grade labour. But it is clear that it will be some considerable time before they are serious possibilities. And even after that point is reached, it is uncertain how long it would take until they are in widespread application, and no longer just a laboratory curiosity.

For new employment opportunities in the near future, it is clear that we must look at established technology and new developments from it. There are three possibilities which could have a substantial impact. The first is the discovery of oil and natural gas in the North Sea, which command general interest but not enough attention for its possibilities for employment. *The Economist*, in its article 'Texas of the North' of January 29th, 1972 criticised the Government for failing to draw attention to the thousands of jobs that North Sea oil, in particular, was likely to bring to some of the poorest parts of the country, from Scapa Flow to Teeside.

The second possibility is the third London Airport. Apart from the very substantial work involved, both on the airport itself and the necessary infrastructure, there will also be the substantial employment provided by the airport when operational. This obviously will take some time to build up.

The third item is the Channel Tunnel, and coupled with it the additional port development stimulated by EEC entry. An example of this could be the Ocean-Span development, which has been suggested for the Lower Clyde.

A further factor likely to have considerable impact on

MAJOR BREAKTHROUGHS IN TECHNOLOGY*

Forecast by a panel of 20 experts in a study conducted at the Rand Corporation by Dr Olaf Helmer and T. J. Gordon

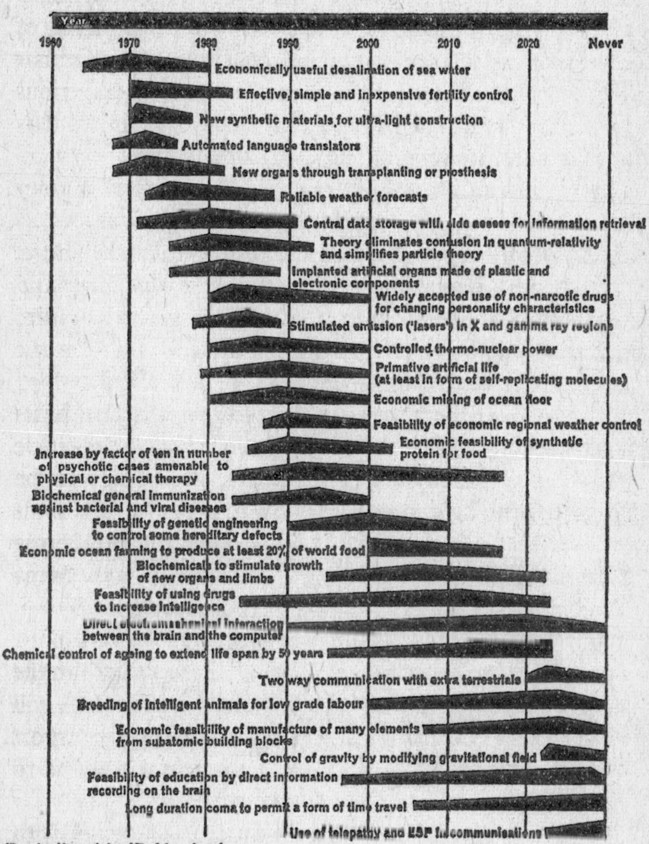

*Reproduced by permission of The Science Journal.

the levels of unemployment is the readiness of the working population to cope with new technologies. Increasingly, in the future, people may have to learn as many as three different skills during their working life. This is one area where it is clear, for all the recent improvements that have been made, we still have a considerable way to go. German industry spends 5 per cent of its payroll on education and training and has approximately 200,000 people in further-training and retraining. (The German government is also spending £200m. on rehabilitation for handicapped people) There are at present nearly 20,000 British workers in Germany and from there it is possible to make direct comparisons between workers from the two countries. A comment to be heard in Germany is that a skilled worker, by British standards, is not sufficiently skilled for German companies. The Germans are said to be trained with a much broader general basis leading to specialised training in a particular field. By contrast the whole British apprenticeship system in the craft trades has led to a much narrower training and one less able to embrace new technologies that are introduced. For example, the German engineering industry works on the module system of training. Admittedly, this system is now employed by the Engineering Industry Training Board, but it has not of course had time to make any more than an initial impact here.

Two other German developments have considerable bearing on the problem.

The first is the German Employment Promotion Act of 1969. This is a comprehensive measure which includes, in particular, vocational guidance and vocational training incentives, incentives to enter employment, industrial and vocational rehabilitation of handicapped persons, short time allowances, incentives to employment throughout the year in the building industry, programmes for the creation of employment opportunities, particularly creation of employment opportunities for ageing employees. To some extent, this may be a labour-hoarding measure; but some at least of its ingredients should be considered seriously.

The second development is the very substantial pension aims to which Germany is working. The objective is that pensions should reach 75 per cent of a normal salary and also be protected by a form of escalation which is geared to national wealth. This latter is obviously a most important item if there is to be any progress towards earlier retirement.

In considering where new job opportunities may occur, it is also important to consider who is going to create them. There are many examples over the years where individual entrepreneurs have been the quickest to realise the possibilities in new technology and to exploit them.

In recent years however, the main activities of entrepreneurs have often not been so much the exploitation of new technologies as the exploitation of rationalisation in existing industries. If the industrial 'folk hero' of earlier years was Lord Nuffield, his successor may be Mr Jim Slater. It could be argued that he has hardly created any jobs but has built his empire by going in the opposite direction. And many of the brightest and most ambitious of the current generation are busily trying to follow his example.

The efficient use of assets is undoubtedly desirable: but the tax thicket tends to leave the creative entrepreneur and the manager at a disadvantage compared with the city men who can direct much of their labour to extracting the best from the system. It is to be hoped that the fiscal system can progressively redress the balance. Nevertheless the area of employment which seems to offer the greatest scope for increased employment may not be industry, but the social services – principally health, welfare, social security, education and the prison and probation services.

There is a clear abundance of needs to be met. Better geriatric, psychiatric and disability services; expanded community care; shorter hospital waiting lists; pre-school education; smaller classes; effective penal services; an attack on the big city slums and social problems; extended family planning services – these are only some of the areas where most people will recognise that there are major social needs which by and large can only be met with an expansion of the manpower of these normally labour-intensive services. We certainly have no doubt that a fair proportion of the greater wealth which we hope to see generated should go towards them. We want to see the market economy doing still more to help the social sphere.

At the same time, it is evident that even on existing levels of provision, a steady expansion in social service jobs is under way. In *Social Trends No. 2* (HMSO) Dr S. Rosenbaum of the Central Statistical Office has an important article on 'Social Services Manpower'. He points out that the proportion of dependent groups (children and those over retirement age) to those of working age is increasing steadily; and he concludes that if present trends continue, the result may be a 3½ per cent per annum increase in social service manpower over the five years from 1970 to 1975. 'On this basis the total manpower requirements of the social services will grow from just under 2 million in 1970 to over 2·3 million in 1975 in terms of full-time equivalent'.

Coming at a time when the total working population is expected to remain fairly constant – the female population rising by about 2 per cent, the male falling by about ½ per cent – this could represent a fairly substantial contribution to the employment situation. An increase of this order took place between 1961 and 1966, but this was at a time when the economically active population increased by some 800,000.

Obviously it is too simple to say that 300,000 new jobs in the social services represents 300,000 jobs knocked off the unemployment figure. It is not enough to have people – they must be the right people, with the right qualifications, in the right place. Nevertheless, by aiming at a still higher level of social provision than has been postulated in the past – or in other words, by developing further the improvements launched by Sir Keith Joseph and his colleagues – we can hope to make a real dent in the unemployment level. The overriding need – apart from finance – is clearly a very careful assessment of the relevant manpower and training requirements.

CHAPTER SEVEN

Public works policies

THE PRESENT GOVERNMENT have been rightly appalled by the prevailing levels of unemployment and have taken massive measures aimed at redeeming it. The most notable steps have included reductions in taxation amounting to over £3,000m. in a full year including cuts in Income Tax, Purchase Tax, Corporation Tax and SET. Allowances on capital expenditure have been increased and free depreciation extended in scope. Other demand management action has included increases in Social Security benefits, reductions in Bank Rate, the repayment of Post War Credits and the abolition of hire purchase terms control. The government have also sought directly to stimulate employment by means of accelerating investment in the nationalised industries and in the infrastructure of the assisted areas. Additionally they have also brought forward the naval shipbuilding programme, provided finance for the RB 211 engine and made extra provision for road maintenance and for housing improvement grants in the assisted areas.

The expenditure under all these heads totals £900m. but most of it does little to provide the new jobs immediately which should be the aim of an effective public works policy. The root of the problem is the delay between the decision of the government to provide the money and the beginning of the resultant employment. The search for projects, the speeding up of plans, the obtaining of necessary consents, and the final preparatory work are all time consuming stages. Too often the process is not started until unemployment has reached crisis level. The present position illustrates this very clearly since it is a fact that expenditure on local public works projects is limited, not by government's readiness to spend, but by the non-availability of local authority plans. This chapter examines the history of public works programmes and makes some recommendations for improving their capacity swiftly to reduce unemployment. Discussion of such programmes flourished during the 19th and early 20th centuries but has receded in the steadier and less cyclical economic climate of the post World War II era. But now that unemployment has reached a level unprecedented in this period it is hardly surprising that interest in the subject should have suddenly revived, and that the Keynes/Bevin addendum to the 1931 Macmillan report, which argued that 'new capital investment would in present circumstances create additional employment', should be recalled, along with Roosevelt's New Deal.

Despite the fact that in the pre-war period a 'compensatory' public works policy was generally accepted as a principal anticyclical weapon, the achievements of that policy were minimal. Between 1920 and 1931 the Unemployment Grants Committee approved schemes costing £191m. It was calculated that the direct employment resulting worked out at 2500 per million pounds per annum. i.e. £400 per job per annum (the equivalent at to-day's prices would be £1750 per job per annum). This employment seldom exceeded 50,000 men at any one time during two decades while unemployment was running around the 2 million mark. After 1925 the Exchequer contributions to the schemes never exceeded £4½m. in a year. Public works policies have never really made a significant contribution to the reduction in unemployment and could only have done so if the expenditure by both central and local government had been vastly in excess of anything contemplated.

The success of the schemes has also been hampered by the decision of governments to impose a substantial proportion of the cost onto local authorities which, in periods of economic difficulty, are understandably anxious to avoid increases in expenditure which might significantly raise the level of rates.

Although some countries have had success with compensatory programmes, Britain, the United States and Canada seem to have reduced their importance in the economic armoury on the grounds that they lack the necessary flexibility for coping with short term unemployment.

There certainly are formidable, and in Britain as yet unscaled, obstacles to the implementation of effective public works policies. They arise from the difficulties inherent in planning, financing and running such programmes. It is just not possible to have an effective set of schemes if governments wait until unemployment begins to increase before they turn their minds to the planning stage. In these circumstances the time lag inherent in quite modest programmes is such that the impact of the programme on unemployment at the crucial stage of the economic cycle is bound to be minimal. Any effective compensatory action would require a planning stage running into years.

This situation could only be avoided if governments were prepared to have a public works 'conveyor belt' ready stocked with projects, the starting button of which could be pushed at the appropriate moment. This would also mean that the projects themselves could be more carefully tuned to the real needs of the community, rather than being dreamt up in a hurry by public officials anxious to produce a list of projects sufficient to ease the consciences and improve the image of politicians confronted with unacceptable unemployment figures.

One particular advantage of a public works policy is that, used sensibly, it can compensate for the disproportionate impact on the construction industry of the deflationary policies apparently inseparable from some stages of economic management.

A political problem however presents itself. If the 'conveyor belt' projects are discussed and planned and are of more than a very low level of social utility, pressures are bound to develop for them to be immediately implemented rather than held for compensatory action. However, it ought technically to be possible with the advance information available to governments on future activity, particularly in the construction industry, to anticipate rather than simply react to a downturn in demand for labour. Indeed, if the construction part of the programme is to rest mainly on the private sector, anticipation is essential when we remember the various planning stages which have to be completed before work can begin. The implementation lag can be reduced if, for instance, a large-scale minor works programme for schools, hospitals and other public buildings rather than a few large projects is undertaken. Planning time lags and the difficulties of co operation between national and local governments also inhibit swift reaction. Moreover, governments have been loath to make advance financial provision for compensatory programmes for either their planning or their implementation.

CONDITIONS FOR AN EFFECTIVE POLICY

The long delays and subsequent ineffectiveness which have in the past characterised public works programmes stem partly from institutional difficulties. If we are to have an effective future plan in this field it would be essential that the government should establish a Compensatory Employment Unit which would have the responsibility for planning and financing the conveyor belt and be ready to start it at an appropriate moment.

If a compensatory works programme is to be effective it must be an integrated part of an overall national approach to the problems of employment and social security. For instance, wherever possible the jobs created should offer ongoing prospects to the unemployed. 'Job creation programmes should place the members of disadvantaged clienteles into 'ladder situations' which provide opportunity for upward progress if the individual continues to achieve personal growth and development.' (*Report on Programmes and Policies of Job Creation.* Ross and Aller 1965 USA).

This must mean that much more imagination than hitherto would need to be applied to a programme and it would have to place less emphasis on construction work. In Germany, Sweden and Canada forestry has played an important role but in this country there is not much scope for land development work with the possible exception of reclamation, rehabilitation and pollution control. There must, however, be very large scope for compensatory employment in the supplementary public services such as the special analysis and up-dating of public records, social surveys, hospital aid and generally tackling with a variety of skills the inevitable backlog of work which builds up in the public sector during periods of excess demand for labour. The Works Project Administration in the USA analysed 285 types of projects including the use of most known trades, skills and professions. In Germany in 1964 over 3,000 white collar workers were engaged in libraries, museums and public offices under the Compensatory Employment Programme in West Berlin alone.

There is scope, too, for schemes in the fields of education and health care where shortage of labour is the norm for most of the economic cycle. The wide range of skills which can be absorbed by a supplementary public service programme is given by the breakdown of projects and persons employed in pre-War Works Project Administration in the USA.

TABLE TWENTY-THREE

PERCENTAGE DISTRIBUTION OF PERSONS EMPLOYED ON PUBLIC SERVICE PROJECTS IN THE UNITED STATES

(According to skill, 27th December 1939)

		Project wage employees					
Type of project	*Grand total*	*Total*	*Unskilled*	*Intermediate*	*Skilled*	*Professional and technical*	*Project supervisory employees*
Total service projects	100·00	96·9	52·4	24·8	12·6	7·1	3·1
Public activities	100·00	95·5	16·8	30·1	27·1	21·5	4·5
Research and records	100·00	96·1	18·3	51·0	20·3	6·5	3·9
Welfare	100·00	97·7	76·6	15·1	4·5	1·5	2·3
Other	100·00	97·7	73·2	15·9	7·0	1·6	2·3

Source: Federal Works Agency: *Final Report on the WPA Program* (Washington D.C., Government Printing Office, 1947), p. 38.

Incidentally, it is calculated that of the total costs of WPA projects from 1935–41 no less than 85 per cent represented labour costs.

Compensatory employment programmes should concentrate on the longer term unemployed. In a mobile work force such as ours (8 million job changes per annum), backed with wage related unemployment benefit and redundancy benefits, short-term unemployment is not too serious. Indeed, if it leads to better use of resources it may be of positive economic value.

A Swedish parliamentary commission has warned against placing the unemployed too quickly into emergency works programmes. It is not easy to establish what the 'qualifying period' ought to be. The period of 'frictional' (or what might be called routine) unemployment varies from skill to skill, industry to industry and winter to summer; but an analysis of UK unemployment from 1961–65 showed that if the number of registered unemployment remained constant at 400,000, half the people on the register at any one time could be expected to leave within ten weeks (*Ministry of Labour Gazette* – April 1966). However, six to eight weeks out of work would be enough to justify the offer of training or compensatory employment on grounds of morale and social and economic cost.

Because of the difficulty of persuading local authorities to take on financial burdens in a difficult economic climate in order to start public works programmes, such schemes ought to be overwhelmingly centrally financed. This probably means borrowing, since in the expansionary climate likely to be prevailing in the monetary and fiscal spheres debt is likely to be cheap to finance. Assuming a target of 150,000 to 200,000 in compensatory employment programmes, at periods of peak unemployment, we would have to be prepared to face expenditure of up to £400m. p.a.

There is one special problem to be faced: the risk that even with high unemployment, one may run into particular bottle-necks. Ever since the war, one important constraint on British industry has been shortages of particular skills. Of course some occupations are always short – nursing and public transport notoriously so; but the main concern is with those areas of activity within which the balance between supply and demand fluctuates according to the general economic climate. These shortages are most likely to manifest themselves in a period of expansion following one of stagnation. The labour market is notoriously slow to respond to such revivals, and bottle-necks have been especially severe and recurrent in the skilled engineering and construction industries.

Although the Department of Employment in 1970 made a special study of skilled engineering shortages in Leicester (*Skilled Engineering Shortages in a High Demand Area*) and NEDC is currently considering the whole question of bottle-necks, precise statistical information on these situations is difficult to acquire. The figures which are available reflect only the broad national scene and give no true representation of the present situation where, despite a million unemployed, severe shortages of, for instance, bricklayers are still experienced in some areas of the country.

Such shortages may clearly hold up the implementation of public works policies. They also have another implication. Some of them undoubtedly occur because of a drift of skilled men away from some occupations or perhaps even from this country in periods of recession. To the extent that compensatory programmes could give opportunities for skilled workers to continue in relevant employment during such periods, they should tend to decrease this drift. Improved employment placement policies are anyway needed to contribute by swifter matching of men to vacancies. If at the same time as we develop compensatory employment programmes and improve placement services we can link the government's improved training scheme into an accurate manpower intelligence system better able to forecast future shortages, we ought to be able to make significant progress in eliminating many of the most difficult bottlenecks. At the very least, we need a close look at the way in which these things are being tackled in Whitehall. It is no good simply saying that reflation will take care of the whole problem.

To sum up then, we believe that public works policies can contribute more constructively than in the past to reductions in cyclical unemployment. If they are to do so however, we need a more concerted approach. We should as a start establish a Compensatory Employment Unit within the Department of Employment responsible for the total programme and charged with the bringing together of a list of projects covering as wide a span of skills as possible, heavily weighted towards the more easily initiated 'minor works' end of the scale.

CHAPTER EIGHT

The right to work

EVER SINCE THE WAR, full employment and the right of every man to a job have been generally accepted as social and political objectives. There has not been very much argument about what exactly they imply, for the simple reason that there has not needed to be much argument about them: the jobs for the most part have been there. We may not have been steadily in the situation which Beveridge postulated of a regular surplus of jobs over workers; but year in, year out the talk has been at least as much of labour shortages as of labour surpluses. Only in some of the regions like Ulster, the North East and Scotland has there been a persistent unemployment problem.

Today, however, improved productivity and structural changes make it likely that the number of manhours required to operate even an appreciably more buoyant productive industry than we have at the moment will be smaller than it has been in the past. Some of the slack can certainly be taken up in other forms of employment. Other ways of using the 'manhour surplus' are considered elsewhere in this pamphlet. But this does not absolve us from the need to think about the possibility that for an indefinite period there may simply be fewer jobs to go round. How does this possibility match up with the right to work?

This raises some tricky issues. Assuming that – as we should – we stick to the objective of full employment, we must still ask ourselves the following questions. Do we believe in keeping people in jobs that are not economically justified; in other words, should industry be used as a branch of the social services? To what extent should we be prepared to distort the economy to solve the special problems of employment in the regions? Do we consider that women should in all circumstances have exactly the same right to a job as men? Is it morally, as well as economically, justified compulsorily to lower the age of retirement? Should we insist on people moving if necessary to seek work? Should we increase the pressure on people to seek different forms of work, if work in their own employment is not available? Do we do enough to ease occupational change? Or should we perhaps say that if some people don't seem all that keen to work when there is an overall shortage of jobs, why worry too much about them? Equally, at the lower end of the pay scale, is there enough *point* in working; does not the present pattern of earnings, taxes, benefits and rebates act as a disincentive either to seek employment or in some cases to seek better paid employment? And finally, does the right to work entail being handed, as it were, a job on a plate; or may it require a degree of initiative from the work seeker?

These are not new questions; but they have a heightened relevance under the new circumstances.

If one were to define the philosophy that has prevailed since the war, one might say that the notion of full employment has included the objective that people should be provided with the opportunity of work of their choice at the place of their choice. In other words, the payment of unemployment and supplementary benefit has never been dependent on people (except sometimes young unmarried men) moving to work where work is available; nor has it required that people should shift from their usual occupation to another occupation, or to work in their own occupation which is below the normal rate of pay. Nor are unemployment or supplementary benefits withheld from people who refuse to undergo retraining. Insofar as occupational and geographical mobility have been encouraged by official policy, it has been through carrots rather than sticks – grants for people moving to new areas for work and for retraining.

The one thing, of course, that has never been given is the cast-iron guarantee of a job. Without direction of labour, it is doubtful if it ever could be. Beveridge's view, in his 1944 unofficial report on *Full Employment in a Free Society*, was that the government should make sure that there was always a surplus of jobs over workers. Within this framework, however, he was a good deal tougher than post-war governments have ever felt able to be.

Beveridge in fact argued that 'it should be accepted as a general citizen duty that if there is a demand for labour at fair wages, men who are unemployed for any substantial period should be prepared to take that work and not to hold out indefinitely for work in their own trade and place; service means doing what is wanted, not just pleasing oneself. This does not imply that there should be continuance in peace of the powers exercised in war by the Ministry of Labour and National Service. No man should be subject to criminal penalties in peace for refusing work however unreasonably. But he should not be assisted to be unreasonable by provision of an insurance income. A just consequence of a full employment policy would lie in the stiffening of the conditions of unemployment benefit as regards individuals whose unemployment continues for any length of time'. Later on, he says that 'Mobility of labour does not mean perpetual motion. Mobility of labour means merely that labour should be capable of moving and ready to move if necessary.'

The tendency of post-war governments of both parties to take a tenderer view about mobility than Beveridge implied has not only derived from the failure to achieve a persistent surplus of jobs over people. It has been due on the one hand to a sociological awareness that the breaking up of communities is distasteful to those who constitute them and may lead to the social hazards that can spring from loss of roots; and on the other hand to recognition that to shift people from areas where schools, houses and other services exist (even if sometimes at a poor level) to, say, the rapidly growing South East may not make very good economic sense. The general philosophy of moving jobs to people rather than people to jobs has a good deal to be said for it.

This is not to say that where people are willing to move, they should not receive encouragement. The Department of Employment discussion paper *Training for the Future* states in paragraph 114 that there will be a new scheme of more generous financial assistance for those who after re-training have to move in order to get a job. We consider such assistance to be vital, though we accept that if *too* many of the livelier and more able members of a community move elsewhere, that community may be impoverished.

Certain private companies have devised good transfer schemes. One company had to re-organise its distribution network in the UK which involved closing down many depots and building thirteen new ones. It produced an excellent booklet for the staff involved. This described the towns where the thirteen new depots were to be built and included such information as house availability, rents, rates, shopping facilities, schools, churches, entertainments, play groups, job opportunities for wives, sporting facilities. A real attempt was made to put over the attractions of the towns where the depots were to be located.

In addition to this there was a generous scheme for house purchase mortgages and removal assistance. Where an employee moved to a new town selling his old house and buying a new one the following costs were met:

(*i*) All legal fees in respect of sale, purchase and mortgage.

(*ii*) Estate agents fees for selling the employees house.

(*iii*) Survey fee (for one house only).

(*iv*) Furniture removal costs.

(*v*) 12 per cent of the employees gross annual salary or basic wage as a lump sum towards disturbance costs.

(*vi*) A grant of £20 per head for each dependant (excluding wife).

Bridging loans for deposits were also available.

Any State scheme would have to have some of these elements in it, as well as providing for the possibility of the worker buying his house; there would also have to be a positive effort to ease transfers of council tenants. The March White Paper *Industrial and Regional Development* in fact promises an improved Resettlement Transfer Scheme.

Since the war, a variety of regional policies have been tried. It is not the purpose of this chapter to analyse them in detail; but overall it cannot be said that all or any of them have proved capable of more than holding the relative regional position. Moreover, governments have been exposed to the constant temptation of using industry as a branch of the social services, by keeping uneconomic jobs in being. Whatever the short-term political and social attractions of that may be, in the long term it can only contribute to the overall relative economic decline of Britain.

Does this mean that regional policies should be scrapped? No: they should be judged on their merits. The next chapter puts forward a possible approach. But the key to success in at least some of the regions surely lies in getting away from the notion that 'they' – i.e. Whitehall or big business – must provide jobs, as it were, on a plate, to some greater feeling within the people of the region that much of the initiative in providing new jobs must come from them. Perhaps the greatest economic weakness in say the Northern region is a dearth of home grown entrepreneurs and managers. A very interesting study by Professor J. W. House and some colleagues from Newcastle University on *The Mobility of the Northern Business Manager* brings out the sheer shortage of managers in that part of the world (as well as such specific problems as the lack of what some managers think of as a stimulating environment, adequate schools for their children and so on). The old industries simply seem to have had too high a proportion of 'other ranks' to 'officers'. Where new *entrepreneurs* have launched businesses in that part of the world, they have tended to come from outside.

It may be that there was something in the nature of the old industries that produced a high level of solidarity among those who worked in them but a low level of economic initiative. The natural working class leaders gravitate to the trade unions and even Parliament, rather than seeking to become bosses in their own right.

It is easier to analyse, or at least to speculate, than to dispose: but the fact is that modern industry, particularly with its consumer orientation, seems to need an adjustability and responsiveness that does not appear to grow naturally in the rather inflexible environment of the coalfields and shipyards. But unless areas like the North can breed their own creators of wealth, they will continue to be prone to the besetting difficulty of regional policies that when production is reduced it is the regional outposts of the large companies that suffer first.

The corollary to geographical stability as opposed to mobility, in the regions, is, then, less dependence on government and industry outside in the creating of new jobs. It is also more rapid *occupational* mobility.

Here Beveridge's 'general citizen duty' has more to be said for it: the case for supporting in unemployment those who are not prepared to switch jobs needs re-examining, albeit sensitively. One of the features of the recent period of high unemployment has been the persistent cry 'why is it that I can't get workers for such and such a job (usually skilled or at least semi-skilled) when there are a million unemployed?' Equally, there has been a real fear that the government's very big construction programme would run into trouble because of shortages among various branches of the building and construction trades.

The right way of transferring workers from one industry to another, via retraining, is certainly the carrot rather than the stick, coupled with the carefulness that the coal industry has, to its credit, shown in its handling of redundancies. Although training allowances are now up to £5 per week above the unemployment benefit level, it may well be that the incentive needs to be further stepped up. But at the end of the day it seems reasonable to insist that someone who has been out of work for some substantial period of time should either move into a new occupation, or receive the training which would equip him to move into a new occupation.

To be fair, this is a greater problem among the skilled than the unskilled. There the present system is that if an unskilled worker cannot find work in his usual occupation, he may after a time be required to accept more or less comparable work. An unskilled person might be required, for example, to accept employment as either a labourer or a kitchen porter or a garage attendant. It has, at the same time, always been recognised that the unemployment total contains a proportion of those least capable of working – the near unemployables in fact – but men or women who cannot be precisely distinguished or labelled like the physically disabled. With managements' more critical attitude to the quality of its labour force and with overall an increase in the level of intelligence required for jobs in modern industry this proportion is likely to increase. Despite the low potential of their economic contribution society cannot shrug off these men not least because of the dangers that prolonged idleness of a large number of such people could breed. A special government study is needed.

For most of the unemployed, then, coercion would serve little purpose, and the carrot equally have little appeal. On the other hand, we need to keep a close watch on what is happening at the point where unemployment and supplementary benefits rub shoulders with low wages. There is some reason to believe that we have got to a stage where the incentive to find work or increase one's earnings is altogether too low – thanks to a combination of benefits, rebates and taxation. The government's policy of selectivity made very good sense in the circumstances in which it was introduced: Family Income Supplement, higher remission of health and welfare charges, the new housing rebates and rent allowances are all sensible ways of directing resources to meet needs: but their overall effect, coupled with the crossing of the tax threshold, is liable to act as a disincentive. If we want people to work, and work effectively, we must make it worth their while. It must surely be the strategy of phase two of the socio-economic policy of this government to stimulate a switch back from dependence on benefits to dependence where possible on earnings, with a real expectation that someone of working age will be clearly better off in work than out of it. In this context, retraining should be equated with being in work.

Since something like a third of the lowest paid tenth of the male population, and nearly as much in the lowest paid quarter, are in the public sector, the government's ability to shuffle round with wage rates, benefits and tax is substantial. Even leaving the tricky question of wages and differentials on one side, there must be scope for a deliberate policy of reducing tax and benefits in parallel among those who have reached the tax threshold.

This chapter does not cover all the questions raised at its beginning: the position of women and the possibility of early retirement and shorter working hours, as well as the regional question are considered elsewhere. But what it does seek to do is to suggest that we should look more closely at the ways in which we spur on some of the unemployed to take up work. Geographical mobility of labour should be very much a voluntary matter, but occupational mobility needs more positive encouragement. The mere provision of extra training places will not in itself be enough, even if it is accompanied – as we must hope – with a strong likelihood that there is a job to be found when the training is done. At the same time, it is no good pretending that most jobs are going to lie awaiting picking like ripe fruit, or that government alone can meet employment needs, either by directly providing work or through sophisticated demand management. Important though these both are, the making and seizing of entrepreneurial opportunities is equally vital. The right to work entails obligations on the part of both workers and on those who create the climate within which industry can thrive or wilt.

CHAPTER NINE

Working women

ANY STUDY OF employment today is bound to look at the place of women in it. It must be said that the picture is brighter than for men, even if there are uncertainties in it. The total number of women in employment in this country is rising steadily and has been throughout the last decade. Not only are the total numbers steadily increasing but the percentage of the female population who are economically active has shown a consistently rising trend. As Table 24 shows, women have made up an ever increasing percentage of the total working population not only of Great Britain as a whole but in every part of the country.

Employment estimates for regions* have been made quarterly since June 1965 and the latest are for March 1971. Before June 1965, estimates were made only for each mid-year. Table 24 shows information for each June from 1961 to 1970 and for March 1971.

This increase in the number of women in employment and the rising proportion that they represent of the total working population has been consistently under-estimated every time that an official forecast of the total working population has been attempted in recent years. There is no reason to believe that the increase in the female working population is going to slow down at all in the years ahead.

There has, in fact, been a slight fall in the economic activity rate of women in the age groups 25 to 39. This is undoubtedly the result of earlier marriage and child-

*The present standard regions were introduced in April 1965. For June 1964 and earlier dates, employment estimates are available for South East and East Anglia, and for East Midlands and Yorkshire and Humberside collectively but not separately.

TABLE TWENTY-FOUR

ESTIMATED NUMBERS OF FEMALE EMPLOYEES IN EMPLOYMENT

expressed as percentages of all employees in employment

	June 1961	*June 1962*	*June 1963*	*June 1964*	*June 1965*	*June 1966*	*June 1967*	*June 1968*	*June 1969*	*June 1970*	*March 1971*
South East					37·5	38·3	38·5	38·6	38·9	39·3	39·2
East Anglia					34·8	34·5	34·7	35·3	36·2	36·6	37·7
South East and East Anglia	37·0	37·1	37·2	37·4	37·4	38·0	38·2	38·4	38·7	39·1	39·1
South West	34 0	34·5	34·6	34·9	35·3	35·7	36·0	36·4	37·3	37·4	37·7
West Midlands	35·3	35·4	35·4	35·7	35·7	35·8	36·0	36·5	36·8	37·0	36·9
East Midlands					35·0	35·8	35·9	36·2	36·6	37·4	37·2
Yorkshire and Humberside					35·4	35·8	36·0	36·6	36·9	37·3	36·9
East Midlands and Yorkshire and Humberside	34·7	34·6	34·6	34·8	35·3	35·8	35·9	36·4	36·8	37·4	37·0
North West	38·0	37·8	37·6	37·9	38·2	38·5	38·4	38·8	39·1	39·3	38·7
North	31·5	31·9	32·5	33·0	33·5	34·0	34·6	35·7	36·5	36·9	36·5
Wales	29·7	30·2	30·4	31·2	32·1	32·7	32·8	33·7	34·2	35·0	36·0
Scotland	36·1	36·3	36·7	36·8	37·3	37·8	38·0	38·7	39·1	39·4	39·7
Great Britain	35·7	35·9	35·9	36·2	36·4	36·9	37·1	37·5	37·9	38·3	38·2

TABLE TWENTY-FIVE

FEMALES REGISTERED AS UNEMPLOYED

expressed as percentages of all persons registered as unemployed at September each year

	1961	*1962*	*1963*	*1964*	*1965*	*1966*	*1967*	*1968*	*1969*	*1970*	*1971*
South East	25·9	24·3	22·5	22·2	18·8	17·8	15·2	14·0	13·6	12·9	13·9
East Anglia	23·4	23·3	25·4	24·4	21·9	18·5	18·9	15·4	16·2	14·1	15·1
South West	25·9	25·4	24·6	23·7	21·6	20·1	18·2	17·2	16·6	15·9	17·2
West Midlands	24·5	25·3	25·2	28·7	27·3	23·2	17·6	15·9	13·7	13·4	11·5
East Midlands	28·9	27·3	25·3	25·2	22·3	20·1	18·5	14·7	14·3	15·5	15·4
Yorkshire and Humberside	27·9	26·6	26·2	27·0	24·7	22·0	18·6	14·3	15·6	14·3	15·5
North West	30·8	30·4	29·3	24·9	24·5	23·6	20·8	14·9	14·2	14·0	16·0
North	24·2	23·7	24·0	24·4	23·1	20·7	18·7	15·2	15·8	16·4	17·4
Wales	27·1	27·1	28·3	30·0	27·0	24·9	23·6	19·0	18·3	17·8	20·3
Scotland	28·4	26·7	27·8	28·6	28·0	24·5	25·3	20·7	19·0	18·7	19·5
Great Britain	27·2	26·4	26·0	25·7	23·8	21·7	19·4	16·0	15·5	15·1	15·8

bearing. But this decline in the activity rate of younger women has been more than offset by the continuation of the long-term trend towards higher activity rates at the ages 40 to 59. The social trends in the country are for women to marry at an earlier age and for many of them not to stay in employment whilst their children are young. It is becoming an established social practice for women to return to resume full-time careers once their children are of an age that constant domestic attention is not required. It is reasonable to forecast that the main change in this social pattern will come within the next few years when the extension of pre-school and nursery schooling really gets under way. It can only be a matter of time before the intensive all-party lobbying for the provision of state pre-school education as a matter of right achieves success and this will almost certainly boost the number of younger women taking up employment when their children are still extremely young.

It is not perhaps so often realised that the number of job opportunities for women seems to be becoming steadily more numerous and that women have been far less seriously affected by the unemployment problems of recent years. There is always a difficulty in assessing the unemployment level of women because very many women who would take work if it was available do not register as unemployed and do not appear in any official statistics. Nevertheless, this substantial under-estimate of the number of women who would take employment if it were offered and who are not registered as unemployed must have been a constant factor in all official figures for many years past. It is startling to see, therefore, in Table 25, how dramatically the percentage of women in the registered unemployed in Great Britain as a whole and in each of the regions has declined over the last decade.

Table 25 can only indicate that the climate for female employment has steadily improved in relation to that for male employment in every part of the country.

There is also some evidence to show that not only are women a consistently declining percentage of those persons registered as unemployed but that those who are so registered have much less difficulty in finding employment. A ready example of this can be found in the figures for the Nottingham and district employment area over the last two or three years. This is an area which ought not to contain any specially distorting or exceptional regional factors. In October 1971 the unemployment level was 3.4 per cent but male unemployment was 4.8 per cent and female unemployment was 1.1 per cent. More significant is the fact that for every half year over the past three years there have been more unfilled vacancies for women and girls notified to local employment exchanges than unfilled vacancies for men and boys. Most startling of all is the fact that of the 7,030 men registered as unemployed in that area on October 1971, 44.9 per cent had been so registered for less than three months whereas 45.1 per cent had been registered for more than three months. The equivalent percentage for the 823 women so registered were 70.3 per cent registered for less than three months and 29.7 per cent for more than three months. In the generally difficult employment position in Nottinghamshire at that time, the brightest feature was a constant demand for all classes of skilled female workers, particularly machinists, in the clothing industry in the area. The most extreme localised example of the contrast between male and female employment positions in the county was in a mining town – Hucknall – where a shirt manufacturer was running an intensive publicity campaign to attract women back into employment following the opening of a day nursery catering for the children of employees. At the same time some redundancies had been declared at the local colliery mainly for men in the over 55 age group who had no opportunity of alternative work.

It is dangerous to draw hard and fast conclusions from such localised examples particularly when it is impossible to obtain an equivalent picture of the overall national position. Nevertheless, there are some indications in the national figures that this is not a wholly isolated or unusual situation. Turning to Table 24 above, the biggest increases in the percentage of women in employment appear to have taken place in the North, Wales, and Scotland which are all development areas. Those three areas, it is true, all had the highest percentage of women registered as unemployed, in Table 25, but this merely indicates that if the increase in female employment opportunities in those areas continues there is no sign of any drying-up of supply of women to take them.

Very little study seems to be taking place of the social difficulties that this can create in those places where the traditional balance between male and female employment is being changed. Inevitably there must always be some places where the proportion of men to women amongst those seeking work will not match exactly the proportion of male and female jobs. There are indications, however, that the number of such places is increasing. It is only too likely that this will happen in areas where there is a decline in employment in traditional heavy industry and an influx of new light industry employing large numbers of women machinists.

It is true of course that many female jobs in industry are in packaging or in assembly and inspection work on the production line and this type of work is likely to be mechanised at an accelerating rate; but this has not produced any noticeable effect on the imbalance of the job opportunities so far.

At the very least there must be a serious possibility that the employment position in depressed regions will improve more slowly when the jobs in newer industry being attracted to those regions are more readily suitable for women than for men, and there is an ever increasing number of women who want to take such jobs and will therefore keep men out of the new employment.

Most aspects of this trend are, of course, welcome in that they reflect the growing emancipation and career and job opportunities for women. Nevertheless, it must be one of our conclusions that this trend should not be sustained artificially by those measures which increase the advantages for women over men when seeking work. It underlines the need to ensure that the Equal Pay Act when it comes into force is made effective in practice so that the growing army of women in work are not drawn in because they provide a source of cheaper labour. Of course if equal pay, and other costs, could be established then assuming no skill or aptitude differences for certain jobs, women would stand at a disadvantage due to their less good absentee record – a regular 10 per cent or so – and the uncertainty in the employment of younger women created by the consequences of marriage. Similarly, it is to be hoped that those provisions of the Industrial Relations Act which give every employee the right to Trade Union membership, and every registered Trades Union the right to recognition in accepted circumstances, become effective so far as female employees are concerned because there are undoubtedly some employers who prefer a female labour force to a male one because it tends to be less 'unionised' and certainly far less militant. All differences in the rates of national insurance contribution and the pension benefits of men and married women must also be removed when the Government undertakes its large scale reform of our pensions structure.

Finally, the Government ought to begin some study of the dangers of imbalance between male and female employment opportunities in particular areas of the country, and consider whether more thought ought not to be given to this aspect when considering applications for industrial development certificates and other aspects of regional policy. This conclusion is merely underlined by our forecast, elsewhere in this pamphlet, that the social services are the sector of the economy most likely to provide new employment opportunities over the next few years, as the proportion of women to men employed in this field can be expected to be particularly high.

CHAPTER TEN

A regional approach

Since the chapter below was written, the Government has made major organisational and financial changes to its regional policy. Nevertheless, it was felt worthwhile to include it in its original form as a number of the proposals set out below have either been implemented in the new policy or are still very relevant to the continuing problem of regional unemployment.

A final paragraph has been added to include some comments on the Government's new policies.

Discussions on regional policy sometimes assume that the problems of economic disparity between one part of the United Kingdom and another are relatively new, whereas, of course, basic shifts in population, employment and income have been evident in British history ever since the trends were first recorded. In 1700, one-third of the British population lived in seven counties in the South and West. The main areas of population density were around London, Bristol and Exeter – in the Eastern counties – Lancashire and the West Riding; with Worcestershire as the most densely populated county in the country.

The growth of industry in the early nineteenth century around the coal fields and near the ports led to the pre-eminence of Lancashire, the West Riding, central Scotland and the hinterland of the Tyne, Wear and Tees. In the time span of history, however, the major importance of these industrial areas was relatively short-lived. By the end of the nineteenth century, the development of more complex products than the old staple industries of coal, iron and steel, textiles and shipbuilding, demanded an agglomeration of small engineering companies producing assembly items, and the birth of the great consumer industries enhanced the trend of locating these new industries in areas near the richer and larger markets of London and the Midlands.

It is possible to trace the beginning of the problems of Scotland, the Northern Region and Wales to the end of the nineteenth century, and the failure of these areas to attract replacement industries from that time has brought about a cumulative process of decline. Other areas in the country such as the North West, Yorkshire, Humberside, East Anglia and the South West had problems too, but not of such a severe kind. What it is possible to say, is that in the twentieth century, the South East has done nothing more than recover its traditional pre-eminence in the national economy – a pre-eminence which it has held ever since the Middle Ages with the exception of a short period in the last century.

The disparity in employment levels first encouraged major national attention, on social grounds, in the inter-war years. Yet, although Government intervention dates from the 1930s, major policies have only been focused on those problems for the past decade, so that it may be a little premature to draw firm conclusions on the effectiveness of Government action over the period. There can be little doubt, however, that, left alone, the imbalances would have been self-correcting in the course of time, and although the social upheavals from non-intervention by the Government might have been more severe, the attraction of modern replacement industries might well have been faster. As it is, the effect of the policies of the past decade has been to encourage, or to force through the

IDC system, new industries into these areas, which are not necessarily suited to the environment concerned.

It is unwise to generalise from particular examples, but the experience of the engineering Company A shown in Chapter Three is informative. Its plant in a development area has been supported by heavy subsidy, yet its relevant competitive position beside its sister plant in the Midlands has declined year by year. The figures are re-stated here for interest.

TABLE TWENTY-SIX

COMPANY A

	Midlands plant		**Scottish plant**	
Year	*Av. hourly earnings*	*Output per man hour*	*Av. hourly earnings*	*Output per man hour*
1967	100 (@ 634p)	100	100 (@ 651p)	100
1968	106	111	113	97·3
1969	113	117	123	106
1970	130	126	143	110
1971	144	134	149	114

There are grounds for believing that a major number of the large new industries which have been encouraged to the development areas over the past decade would be making losses if subsidies were to be removed.

Nevertheless, although the whole exercise must be beset by doubts, there seems little purpose in promoting the abandonment of regional policies on economic grounds – although it would certainly be possible to advance respectable arguments to support such a course – when on politico-social grounds, this would prove totally unacceptable to majority public and political opinion. Indeed, the social pressures in these areas, following a withdrawal of regional assistance, might be such as to force any Government out of office. In these circumstances, the purpose of this section is to question whether any radical new departure would create a faster change in the industrial structure of the depressed areas.

The major element in the policies pursued by all Governments since the early 1960s has been a system of centrally-directed investment incentives for private industry, although the present Government has grafted on to this system a series of centrally-directed environmental projects. The policy has been partially successful in creating new jobs, but it has done so at a huge economic cost, and in nearly every area, the number of new jobs created has been insufficient to offset the decline of the traditional industries. In the period between 1960 and 1965, only an average of 9,100 new jobs were created each year in the development areas by a shift of industry from the more prosperous areas of the country to the regions. Even the replacement industries, which have created the new jobs, are themselves under suspicion, not because they are in declining trades, but because the productivity record, the wage levels, Trades Union militancy and transportation problems have placed them in an uncompetitive posture.

The first question to be asked is why should these policies be centrally-directed at all? (Whitehall has no monopoly of wisdom and industrial skill. It has rather less than an average share of energy and the capacity to take commercial risks. The driving forces for better opportunities, conditions and employment well up in the regions themselves. Whitehall is forced to act through political pressures, not because it lives and breathes the aspirations of the regions for a better deal). There is strong reason for believing that if real vigour, energy and enthusiasm is to be put into regional regeneration, it should come from these areas themselves. Yet anyone who has any experience of the frustrations of regional development, as seen from the regions themselves, must know the near impossibility of getting any radical new scheme off the ground, if it does not conform to the centrally-directed pattern laid down by Whitehall.

In this respect, doubts must exist about the viability of the Government's proposals for the Upper Clyde under which £35 m. of public funds have been pumped into what appears to be a sick and declining trade, thereby preventing for many years to come the industrial regeneration of the Upper Clyde. It is hard to believe that an independent group of Scottish industrialists, presented with an equivalent sum of money to spend, would have chosen such a course of action, which may well prove contrary to the long-term interests of the area. In every sense, it is the peoples of the regions who know their problems, and have the motivation to put them right.

Our first recommendation is therefore for an entirely new structure in regional development, so that the decisions are taken at the periphery, where the problems exist, rather than from the centre. In our view, the Regional Economic Development Councils are an unsuitable forum for such a purpose. As presently constituted, they are ineffective pressure groups, and ultimately are no more than the creatures of Whitehall. Since no elected regional Parliaments exist, and since we believe that elected rather than nominated representatives should form the basis of new 'Sub-Regional Development Authorities' (a term used in the recommendations of the TUC), the solution probably lies through the local government structure. A good example was one of the earliest attempts at creating such a mechanism in the early 1960s by Mr Edward Heath, who, while Secretary of State for Trade, Industrial and Regional Development, set up a 'Committee of Six' for regional development in the South West Region which consisted of the elected representatives of the six Councils of the area – Cornwall, Devon, Dorset, Somerset, Plymouth and Exeter.

Without designating what areas the Sub-Regional Development Authorities should cover, but basing them as far as possible upon natural economic areas in conformity with the new boundaries of local government, we feel that such a structure should be created as soon as possible. The important element is that the majority of the members should be elected councillors, nominated by their own councils to the authority, with perhaps the power to co-opt a minority of qualified industrialists and others who might bring specialist knowledge and skills to the work. The co-opted members would, however, be the choice of the elected representatives who would be more likely to know and choose men of spirit and energy than Whitehall, whose preference would traditionally be for aged men of safety, wisdom and experience at the latter end of their careers.

This structure, which would have the enthusiastic support of the regions, bears some resemblance to the spirit of the recommendations recently emanating from both the CBI and the TUC. It is, however, closest to the recommendations of the Scottish Council in their recent memorandum. Where we would differ from the CBI is in their recommendation for a Commission for Regional Development. While a small body of independent men to advise the Minister on priorities is highly desirable, we would see no object in replacing one centrally-directed structure with another, particularly when the ultimate decisions have to be for the minister himself. The real power should be given to the Sub-Regional Development Authorities who might either borrow directly on the market under Government guarantee, or raise their funds directly from the Treasury on a basis not dissimilar to the loan sanction procedure now prevailing for local government schemes.

To a large extent, the policies which should be pursued would rest upon the recommendations of the Sub-Regional Development Authorities, since they may well differ substantially from one area to another. The Government should resist the temptation to lay down closely defined guide lines, which would place the new authorities in a strait-jacket. The whole process of structural change would be to release the imagination and the energies of the regions themselves. Clearly each authority would have to work to an agreed budget, which in total might call upon national resources not dissimilar to the £309m. which was spent on regional development in 1970/1971. However, some authorities might wish to concentrate their funds on infra-structure, others on transport subsidies, others on subsidies to improve the competitive position of indigenous industries, and others on the encouragement of new industries. A detailed study might well show that before the recent political troubles in Northern Ireland, it was the Ulster authorities who, starting with the greatest problem, made the greatest progress. It is interesting to note that it was the Ulster authorities who had the greatest independence of all the regional authorities in the United Kingdom.

There are a number of areas, however, where the Government could act positively without restricting the freedom of action of the new authorities. First, it should make it easier for labour to move to the depressed areas to those parts of the country where the demand for employment is high. There are social obstacles to greater mobility, such as the availability of housing, relations, friends, and known educational facilities. There are also very real economic costs in making a move. Where a wage earner or an unemployed worker in a depressed area has shown that he has found another job elsewhere, he should be eligible for a mobility grant which would not only cover the cost of his move, but also provide him with an incentive to do so. When it is considered that each job in a development area costs several thousand pounds to create, the saving would be very great if a mobility grant of a few hundred pounds persuaded a family to move to an area where the demand for labour was high. Naturally, safeguards would be required to ensure that the grant was needed for a genuine long term move.

The Government should also review the differential between investment in the development and the non-development areas. It is impossible to make an exact comparison between the old system of cash grants and the new system of free depreciation. Nevertheless, set out below are some calculations made by Messrs. H. H. Scholefield and J. R. Franks in a recent issue of the *National Westminster Bank Review*. It will be seen that on a discounted cash flow basis, the new system would appear to offer a narrower differential than the old. For instance, taking a life of twenty years on plant and machinery, and assuming a pre-tax return of 20 per cent, *the after-tax return* is as follows:

TABLE TWENTY-SEVEN

Old system		**New system**	
Non-dev. area	*Dev. area*	*Non-dev. area*	*Dev. area*
18·4%	22·6%	19·1%	20·0%

It does not matter so much whether the Government reduces or increases investment incentives overall, so far as regional development is concerned. The crucial issue is that the forthcoming budget widens the differential so that investment is made commensurately more attractive than at present in development as opposed to non-development areas.

Thirdly, the Government should draw together all the various departmental responsibilities for regional policy under one senior minister. At the present time, authority is dissipated among five Whitehall Departments under no single figure-head. Among the ministers major tasks might be to put some momentum behind the dispersal of Government and quasi-Government offices in the regions.

Finally, any discussion on regional policy would not be complete without reference to our entry into the European Economic Community. The determination of the Commission to end the distortion of competition by the availability of grants, subsidies and interest-free loans to the companies of member states in central European areas is wholly to be welcomed. It is now possible to obtain substantial special subsidies for investment within a few miles of Brussels, Milan and other major industrial cities. These incentives make any positive regional policy ineffective because they narrow differentials with the outlying areas of the Community. The Government of the United Kingdom should press for the ending of subsidies near to the centre of the Community, and even go to the opposite extreme by considering a congestion tax for the Ruhr, the South East of England, Antwerp and the Paris region etc. Most critical of all, however, is the future of the monetary and economic union. If the Government of the United Kingdom accepts the need for a narrowing of foreign exchange margins between the various currencies of the enlarged Community, it is vitally necessary to press for a major Community initiative in the field of regional policy. If exchange rates are to cease to be the natural mechanism for correcting economic imbalance between the member states, the progress towards monetary union will prove impossible without an alternative system for correcting regional disparities on a continuing and substantial scale.

POSTSCRIPT

The Government's recent announcement on Regional Policy, contained in White Paper (Command Number 4942), is greatly to be welcomed. It implements several of the recommendations made above. First, it widens sharply the investment differentials between the development and non-development areas as shown below. These figures are again taken on a discounted cash flow basis and taking a life of twenty years on plant and machinery, and assuming a pre-tax return of 20 per cent, the after-tax return would be as follows:

TABLE TWENTY-EIGHT

Old system (1966-70)		'New' system 1970-1		Proposed 'new' system 1972 onwards	
Non-dev. area	*Dev. area*	*Non-dev. area*	*Dev. area*	*Non-dev. area*	*Dev. area*
18·4%	22·6%	19·1%	20·0%	20·0%	26·5%

These figures will in due course be published in *Accountancy*.

Secondly, it meets the plea for a mobility grant by its proposals for a generous re-settlement transfer scheme and a new re-housing grant of £400. Thirdly, it makes one minister responsible for regional policies with a strong advisory board of experienced individuals drawn from outside Whitehall to support him.

Finally, the Government has gone some way to meeting the major recommendation in the chapter above, namely the opportunity for greater local control in policy making. Regional Industrial Development Boards are to be set up in the assisted areas to advise on investment opportunities and their selection. The Local Employment Act is to be amended to provide a flexible complement to the basic incentives. It is to be regretted, however, that the guide lines exclude any assistance to service industries. In so far as a lingering doubt remains, it is over the degree of autonomy, initiative and financial independence which Whitehall will allow the new Boards. While it is hardly surprising that central government and bureaucracy always resists attempts to dilute its powers, it is still the opinion of the authors of the chapter that the real spirit for a re-generation of the assisted areas must come from the regions themselves.

CHAPTER ELEVEN

In place of work

The burden of this pamphlet has been the serious likelihood that the low levels of unemployment that have characterised most of the post-war period may now be giving way to a period where the sheer quantity of work to be done, in industry at least, is likely to fall substantially. There may be other areas in which some of this shortfall will be taken up – notably, the social services. Equally, some of the present unemployment should disappear as increasing efficiency, coupled with the opportunities offered by the Common Market, allows us to gain new markets and thus stimulate production. It would certainly be folly to land ourselves in the position where we run again into severe labour shortages just at the point where we have a chance to increase output substantially. We cannot after all overlook the fact that other comparable economies, notably Germany's, are still able to continue good productivity with low (if somewhat rising) unemployment.

Nevertheless, we must be prepared for the strong possibility that there will be less work to be done. We reject the view that the right answer to this is to keep industrial jobs permanently in being when their economic justification has gone. In the long run the inefficiency inherent in using industry as a branch of social security can only be damaging. Where government intervenes to keep jobs in being it should only be as a way either of easing their phasing out or of enabling the particular industry to move into economic viability.

This leads to the need for at least some contingency thinking on what to do with the surplus manhours (and womanhours) which are likely to evolve. Oddly enough, this surplus has hitherto been slow to appear. For all the talk about moving into an 'Age of Leisure', an actual decline in the working week has been slow to come about. Some figures quoted in *Social Trends No. 2* are interesting. They show the disparity between the basic hours for male manual workers of twenty-one and over (working full-time) and the actual hours worked, covering the period from 1951 to 1970:

TABLE TWENTY-NINE

	1951	*1961*	*1966*	*1967*	*1968*	*1969*	*1970*
Normal basic hours of work	44·4	42·4	40·4	40·3	40·2	40·2	40·1
Actual hours worked including overtime	47·8	47·4	46·0	46·2	46·4	46·5	45·7

The fall in actual hours worked has been very much less than the fall in basic hours. Nevertheless, there was a significant drop in actual hours worked between 1969 and 1970, and it would be odd if this accelerated trend does not continue.

This chapter therefore seeks to look briefly at various different ways of taking up the slack in such a way that unemployment may be diminished through a degree of work-sharing: the working week and overtime, holidays, age of entering into employment and age of retirement from it.

In approaching these matters, we reject the notion that any sort of work-sharing should be imposed by government. This is partly a matter of political philosophy and partly a belief that evolution in these matters is likely to be much more sensitive and responsive to actual needs and situations than is imposition.

Nevertheless, the government has a role – that of enabling desirable changes to take place and of making sure that they do so without hardship. It also has a responsibility to try to see that any changes do not weaken our international competitive position, particularly as we enter the Common Market.

Over one matter, government or parliament does have direct control: the number of bank holidays. At present, England and Wales have six bank holidays. Against this, Belgium and France have ten, Germany between ten and fifteen (depending on the region) and Italy seventeen.

The case for introducing at least two extra bank holidays is good – indeed so many people already take New Year's Day off that to turn it into a Bank Holiday would be not much more than a switch from *de facto* to *de jure* recognition. However, it is doubtful if an additional day or two of bank holiday would have more than a very minor effect on unemployment.

An increase in normal holidays would clearly have a far more substantial effect. The post-war years have in fact seen a significant increase in holidays. The percentage of full-time manual workers with an holiday entitlement to three or more weeks holiday has risen from one per cent in 1951 to 52 per cent in 1970. (There was a spectacular increase from 15 per cent in 1969 to the 1970 figure) Even though overtime and the coincidence of holidays with slack periods for production will have reduced the effect, this increase must have held down the level of unemployment.

For the most part, however, the increase in holidays has been the result of bargaining rather than statutory based determinations: the exceptions are in industries covered by the wages councils and the Agricultural Wages Acts. By contrast, all except Italy of the EEC countries prescribe minimum annual paid holidays (with France and Luxembourg at the four weeks level, the others lower).

But membership of the EEC does not require that we should follow suit, and it would be a mistake to do so, at least until we have had considerably longer to assess the underlying employment pattern. Far better to allow the trend to continue as it has done in the last few years.

The same principle applies to the length of the working week. It is tempting to argue for positive measures to curb overtime. On the one hand, a good deal of overtime is clearly bogus, in the sense that a reduction of the basic working week and a consequent increase in overtime has been a way of increasing the pay packet. On the other hand, it seems on the face of it unsatisfactory that even at times of high unemployment and short-time working a substantial amount of overtime should still be worked.

In November 1971, for example, 1.6 million workers in establishments with 11 or more employees in manufacturing industries – excluding shipbuilding – (just below 30 per cent of the total) worked overtime, with an average of eight hours a week. The total numbers of overtime hours worked was 13.3 million – equivalent to 332,500 40 hour weeks. By contrast 125,000 workers (just above 2 per cent of the total) were on short-time, with an average loss of 11.7 hours – equivalent to 36,600 40 hour weeks.

Given this situation, it would perhaps be not unreasonable for the union movement to seek to limit overtime by persuading their membership voluntarily to forgo it, so that others might have work. This does not at present seem to be happening to any serious extent, and if it did it would no doubt be accompanied by demands that less overtime should be accompanied by a higher basic wage.

Employers probably have as mixed feelings about overtime reduction as do the unions. Since the days of the famous Fawley productivity agreements, many managements have worked to cut out overtime. Nevertheless, some overtime working represents an efficient use of manpower (as well as a way of satisfying workers). Where overtime meets erratic extra production requirements, it is clearly cheaper than employing extra staff; equally, in some situations it is still anyway impossible to find appropriate extra staff.

In this tangled situation, direct government intervention would be wrong. As a very substantial employer, government should see that it does not use overtime working where the same work could be done efficiently by additional personnel. It should also use its persuasive powers to encourage the nationalised industries and private industry to follow suit. But legislation to ban or curtail overtime is another matter. For one thing, it would sometimes jeopardise economic efficiency; for another it would probably be unworkable and possibly increase the extent of unofficial overtime working, which never reaches the ears of the Inland Revenue. Indeed, there is a school of thought which holds that one way to reduce overtime would be greater noseyness on the part of the Tax Inspectors! The same applies to double-jobbing or moonlighting – a subject which this pamphlet perforce overlooks, due to the almost total lack of concrete information on its extent and nature.

The other side of the overtime coin is, of course, the basic number of hours worked. The post-war trend has been shown in the figures quoted earlier, with the fall in the nominal basic week substantially exceeding the fall in the actual hours worked. Short-time working has not built up to an extent to suggest that it would make sense to offset it by legislating to reduce the working week – even if that was justified on other grounds. What applies in one industry, or one region, does not necessarily apply in another. Anyway, as we have suggested already, it would be foolish at this stage to adopt a policy which necessarily reduces productivity per head. It should, therefore, be for each industry to judge whether it makes sense to reduce its working week or not, or whether alternatively it can divide up its quantum of work among more employees by such measures as four-shift working.

What about the working life?

At the earlier end, there is already in being a seemingly inexorable tendency to delay the point at which education ceases and work starts. The raising of the school-leaving age is the most obvious example of this – and it will, of course, make for an immediate improvement in the employment situation. But the trend goes much further than that. In 1961, 9 per cent of seventeen-year-olds who had been in public sector schools four years earlier were still at school; by 1970, this figure had risen to 17.1 per cent. Similarly, in 1965–66 there were 438,000 students undergoing some form of further education, either full or part-time; by 1969–70 the figure had risen to 590,000 – and the trend again will clearly persist into the future.

All this is entirely to be welcomed – for the non-vocational benefits it will yield, because it should make for a higher quality of workforce and for its impact on the unemployment level. It is when one looks at the other end of the age-range that the problem becomes trickier.

Statistics show that there has been a steady increase in the percentage of men retiring at 65. In 1964 it stood at 57 per cent; by 1969 it had risen to 70 per cent. Similarly, the percentage of men in the 65 – 69 age group who were retired had risen from 73 per cent in 1964 to 80 per cent in 1968.

Nevertheless, a substantial number of men and women of pensionable age remain in work. Among women, over 600,000 remained at work in 1970 after their retirement age of 60. Among men, the figure was 149,000 staying on past their retirement age of 65 – a substantially lower proportion than among women. Between 60 and 65, however, some 1·2 million men were at work.

For human reasons, as well as for the value of much of their work, it would be quite wrong to *impose* earlier retirement. But it is worth thinking carefully about encouraging earlier retirement, and making it more acceptable; and this certainly is an area where the government could act.

This clearly entails making pensions available at earlier ages than 65, and it affects both the State and the occupational pensions systems. Exactly what the cost would be depends on the chosen age and the extent to which people did in fact choose to retire at that age. But some figures given by Mr Paul Dean in the Commons debate of 18th February 1972 on the Holiday Extension and Early Retirement Bill give some idea of the economics of earlier retirement.

According to Mr Dean, the cost of reducing the minimum retirement age for men to 63 would be about £250m. a year (presumably assuming that everyone retired) 'This would mean an increase in contributions ranging from about 2p a week for the £20 a week man to about 25p a week for the £42 a week man' – on the assumption that the increase would be spread between the flat rate and earnings related contributions.

A reduction of the retirement age to 60 would cost no less than £700m. a year, with increases ranging from 5p a week for the £20 a week man, to about 60p for the £42 a week man.

Obviously, the cost of voluntary early retirement would be different, in that many people would continue in work past the age of retirement. But the difficulty of providing for flexibility in the age of retirement is not inconsiderable, particularly as far as the State basic scheme is concerned.

The inevitable corollary of early retirement is simply that the pension paid will be smaller, unless contributions are to increase greatly. As far as the state basic scheme is concerned, an earlier retirement age would almost inevitably entail an increase in the supplementary pension to be paid out. In the private occupational schemes, the cost of providing for a possible extra five years of retirement would be very considerable, unless the level of pension was lowered substantially (and unacceptably).

Nevertheless, the case for facilitating early retirement is strong. For a start, if 50 per cent, of the age group retired at 60, some 600,000 would make way for younger men, with more following in subsequent years up to 65. Moreover, it would take some time before the potential cost of £375m. would be reached, and a fall in unemployment benefit to over-60s would to a limited extent offset this – say by £25m. a year.

Certainly, earlier retirement would not be cheap; but it could bring both economic and social benefits, as well presumably as direct satisfaction to the majority of those who opted for it. On the one hand, it would help to reduce the number of men who are treading water or past their prime in industry and other spheres – not least in the public sector. On the other hand, it would make available many men who are by no means too old to give valuable voluntary or part-time service, or to find new careers in less exacting but still worthwhile occupations. It is worth noting that both Italy and Japan have a male retirement age of 60.

The voluntary retirement age of women could equally be altered if it were thought desirable; and similar considerations would of course apply.

The issue as a whole poses many questions, not least as to what those of retirement age would actually like to do, and are capable of doing. Certainly it would be wrong to tip the scales against their chances of employment where they want employment. Equally, it would be naïve to assume that each job vacated by an older worker would lead automatically to one fewer person unemployed. Any onslaught on unemployment raises problems of matching the right person in the right place to the particular vacancy.

Yet none of this destroys the case for easing earlier retirement; and government, industry and the insurance world should get down to detailed assessment of its possibilities.

CHAPTER TWELVE

Conclusion

This pamphlet is the work of various hands and minds; it lacks therefore the unity and panache of the classic pamphlets. If it has a virtue, it is that a group of Tory MPs of differing experience have thrown into it their knowledge of, and views on, one of the most pressing socio-economic problems of the 1970s – a problem which seems to us a challenge to our whole political and economic philosophy.

And in fact as we have looked at the unemployment trends and ways of meeting them, we have found much common ground among ourselves – enough to sketch the outline of an employment policy for the next decade. Let us try now to summarise it.

For a start, we accept the thesis that, unless action is taken, the low levels of unemployment of the post-war years *may* be a thing of the past. We stress *may;* no one can be sure what will happen, even in the best regulated societies. But at least the evidence of the trends is clear. There has been not only a sharp rise in unemployment; there has also been a steady fall in employment, which is not necessarily the same thing. There has also been a sharp increase in productivity, certainly in 1971, due to a mixture of technological improvement, decay of certain traditional industries and shake-out of labour caused by more efficient management, which sees that a captive labour reserve is no longer necessary for expansion, and the pressure of costs. We have illustrated this trend specifically with evidence drawn from engineering, textiles and other fields. There is a strong likelihood that we are in a quite new situation whose characteristic is faster growth but lower job creation. This general principle is strongly supported by the specific studies reported in Chapter Two and Chapter Three. This trend is at least as likely to apply to white-collar workers as to anyone else. We must face the real prospect of an unemployment level that declines only gradually over the next year or two.

The question is, what do we do about it? First we do not believe that the right answer is to treat industry as a branch of the social services. Keeping jobs in being – or simply creating new ones – to avoid unemployment is bound to lower the long-term rate of growth and competitiveness of British industry. This is as true of the nationalised as of the private sector. There are times when short-term subsidisation makes sense – notably to assist an industry to move towards viability (like cotton some years ago), to contract without hardship (like coal in the 1960s) and perhaps to provide employment in a hard-hit region. But in general defensive policies will never cure our troubles. Instead we must gain new markets and develop existing ones by greater efficiency and competitiveness. After all, economies like the Japanese and the German have shown that high unemployment is not inevitable, and there are huge industrial opportunities ahead if we have the courage to seize them, in energy, transport and many other fields. We need a dose of old-fashioned private enterprise, and the incentives to stimulate it. This embraces company profits as well as individuals' rewards.

It is in this context that our regional proposals must be reviewed. The regions will never thrive if they have to depend on Whitehall for stimulus. They must pull themselves up by their own bootstraps, through their own initiatives, their own decisions.

Anything we do to mop up or use the surplus working

capacity which has grown up in the last few years must avoid making it impossible for industry to increase its labour force if the need should arise: to allow ourselves to be forced back unnecessarily into labour shortage would obviously be folly.

Chapter Elcven of this pamphlet sets out some ideas on how we might absorb much of the surplus manhours with which we are likely to be faced, and let us state clearly that greater leisure is a boon not a burden. Among these ideas, extra holidays, and prolonged education are unlikely to disappear if demand for labour builds up; but the other principal developments – voluntary early retirement (which should be closely examined) and a shorter working week – could clearly be reversed if the demand for labour rose. However, this could essentially be achieved by market forces rather than by government action. Equally, the possible tendency for technological improvements (in production line and packaging type jobs) and equal pay to reduce or contain the amount of industrial work available for women will no doubt be reversed if the demand is there.

It is important not to be naïve about all this. Between the global work force and sufficient people capable of filling particular jobs in particular places there can be a considerable gulf. More and more jobs are going to require specialist training, and even if training can be broadened so that it is a preparation for a wider range of skills than craft training has traditionally provided (perhaps through the modular approach used by the Engineering Training Board) it will never be easy to match people and jobs precisely.

Nevertheless some sort of overall balance should be feasible, if we are prepared to be more positive in our training and retraining policies, and more skilful in forecasting employment needs with more revealing statistical data on the pattern of employment. The Government's recent training proposals represent a good start. So do the new financial encouragements to occupational change. This can come both through incentives to train (making it clearly more rewarding than unemployment) and to move to new employment, and in the last resort by withholding benefit from those who unreasonably decline retraining where it can clearly lead to appropriate jobs. We also need a somewhat tighter attitude towards what is 'suitable employment', with a view to shifting people away from vanishing activities towards those which do and will exist. It really is absurd – as so many people have pointed out – that, at a time of high unemployment, so many jobs which need doing are not being done.

One has only to walk through most big towns to gain an idea of how much squalor persists; or try to find a carpenter or plasterer in many parts of the country; or more important still consider how hard it still is to staff many jobs – skilled and unskilled – in our schools, hospitals and other social services.

Here we come to one of our most positive recommendations: that the government should firmly accept the target of an increase of at least 300,000 jobs between 1970 and 1975 in the social services. Inevitably they will remain labour intensive. They are faced with a continuously rising number of dependants and clients to deal with; and it would be hard to dispute that there is plenty to be done in most of them if they are to meet the continuous revolution of rising standards and aspirations. Both community provision and many of our institutions – geriatric, psychiatric and so on – are crying out for more workers, skilled and unskilled. A very detailed examination of our manpower requirements, and the extent to which they are being met by training, is essential in health, education, social security and the local authority social services.

The need is not only for manpower to staff the public services at the sharp end (as opposed to the bureaucratic end); it is also for manpower to carry out the construction works which form the bulk of any public works policy, as well as the *sine qua non* of many improvements in welfare, health and education. Public works programmes have a chequered history as a means of combatting unemployment, but as an earlier chapter has shown that has been due to their rushed and haphazard nature. A coherent programme or bank of genuinely-needed projects ready in the pipeline could be a very different matter.

It is not however primarily through public works or compensatory employment policies that public funds will create new jobs. There are great ongoing programmes which will be needed, regardless of the unemployment figures. They include most notably the third London Airport, the Channel Tunnel and the exploitation of North Sea Gas.

Our formula then boils down to this: more public spending to meet social needs; more leisure and a shorter compulsory working life: and above all more enterprise in industry and commerce to provide both this essentially welcome leisure and the resources with which our social needs may be met. Some of this will happen of its own accord; some of it will need detailed planning. It is time we got on with the job.

NOTES